"As the drumbeat for racial justice reverberates throughout the United States, Willie Francois charts a course for faithful followers of Christ to move from silent complicity with racism to prophetic resistance. Weaving historical facts, communal witness, and personal experience, Francois calls us to ready our hearts, hands, and minds to usher in a new rhythm for our nation—a rhythm that moves us faithfully toward liberty and justice for all."

—**Leah Gunning Francis**, vice president for academic affairs and dean, Christian Theological Seminary

"With analytical clarity, powerful prose, and a moral-theological vision from which the reader cannot look away, Willie Dwayne Francois III offers Christians and, indeed, *the church* a book that wakes us up and cuts through the static. *Silencing White Noise* is as practical and clear as it is prophetic and courageous; it provides next steps to get—and keep—us moving in the direction on which our lives depend."

—**Jennifer Harvey**, associate provost of equity and inclusion, Drake University; author of *Dear White Christians: For Those Still Longing for Racial Reconciliation*

"Willie Francois III is one of the brightest and most exciting intellectual lights of his generation. In *Silencing White Noise*, he delves into the morass of racial myths that serve to obscure the destructive everyday effects of white supremacy on the lives of Black folks. But just as important, he proposes humane, well-informed solutions to America's racial dilemma. Utilizing insights ranging from contemporary philosophy to theological ruminations to commonsense street logic to contextualized biblical wisdom, this is a brilliant contribution by a brilliant man of biblical faith to the struggle to make America a truly just and humane society."

—**Obery M. Hendricks Jr.**, author of *Christians Against Christianity: How Right-Wing Evangelicals Are Destroying Our Faith*

"An unflinching look at how the white noise of racism keeps us stalled out on the road to a true multiracial democracy and a call to cultivate practices that can get us moving. Francois carefully unpacks how to unlearn racialized habits of mind and replace them with habits of imagination, introspection, and advocacy—the very habits he exemplifies as a preacher, a writer, and a Black church leader. An exquisite blend of theology, storytelling, and history, *Silencing White Noise* is a necessary book."

—**Stephanie Paulsell**, Susan Shallcross Swartz Professor of the Practice of Christian Studies, Harvard Divinity School

"Calling us home to an ethic rooted in the transformative love of inclusion, this work shows us what is possible when we dream of a world with goodness and mercy as its core. In *Silencing White Noise*, Francois demonstrates why he is one of the most important pastoral voices of our generation."

—**Candice Marie Benbow**, author of *Red Lip Theology*

SILENCING
WHITE
NOISE

SILENCING WHITE NOISE

SIX PRACTICES TO OVERCOME OUR INACTION ON RACE

WILLIE DWAYNE FRANCOIS III

Brazos Press

a division of Baker Publishing Group
Grand Rapids, Michigan

© 2022 by Willie Dwayne Francois III

Published by Brazos Press
a division of Baker Publishing Group
PO Box 6287, Grand Rapids, MI 49516-6287
www.brazospress.com

Printed in the United States of America

Library of Congress Cataloging-in-Publication Data
Names: Francois, Willie Dwayne, 1986– author.
Title: Silencing white noise : six practices to overcome our inaction on race / Willie Dwayne Francois III.
Description: Grand Rapids, Michigan : Brazos Press, a division of Baker Publishing Group, [2022]
Identifiers: LCCN 2021057275 | ISBN 9781587435515 (paperback) | ISBN 9781587435652 (casebound) | ISBN 9781493437078 (pdf) | ISBN 9781493437061 (ebook)
Subjects: LCSH: Race relations—Religious aspects—Christianity. | Racism—Religious aspects—Christianity.
Classification: LCC BT734.2 .F725 2022 | DDC 277.30089—dc23/eng/20220120
LC record available at https://lccn.loc.gov/2021057275

The names and details of the some of the people and situations described in this book have been changed in order to protect the privacy of those involved.

Scripture quotations are from the New Revised Standard Version of the Bible, copyright © 1989 National Council of the Churches of Christ in the United States of America. Used by permission. All rights reserved.

The author is represented by the literary agency of Adrienne Ingrum, LLC Agency.

Baker Publishing Group publications use paper produced from sustainable forestry practices and post-consumer waste whenever possible.

22   23   24   25   26   27   28   7   6   5   4   3   2   1

To my son,
I started giving birth to this book a week after your joy-
evoking entrance into our world—a globe jolted by COVID-19,
shutdowns, quarantines, and protests. A boy with many names,
you are called Four, Willie Willie, Nugget, and Peanut.
As you find your own way and make your own name in the
world, may this book help you see the possibilities
of this volatile planet and country where you now reside.

CONTENTS

ACKNOWLEDGMENTS

Sawubona, which literally means "I see you," is a common greeting among the peoples of KwaZulu-Natal in South Africa (when directed to more than one person, it becomes *Sanibonani*). On a moral level, it communicates, "I respect and acknowledge you for who you are." As a response to the greeting, people say *Sikhona*, which literally means "I am here." I want to dedicate these next several lines to express my *Sawubona*.

To my mother, Jacqueline Kennie McClain, and family, for your three and a half decades of affirmations and sacrifices, *Sanibonani*.

To my ancestor, Carolyn Joyce Kennie (my maternal grandmother and memi), for practicing a love for language and literature out loud in my presence, *Sawubona*.

To Dalijah, for handling an uneven share of diaper duties and mealtimes for Willie IV during the writing process, *Sawubona*.

To my peerless literary agent, Adrienne Ingrum, for sharpening my pencil and believing in this work before it ever lived on paper, *Sawubona*.

To Maria Edwards, Utika Byrd, and Rev. Neomi Fletcher, for your stellar administrative work that leaned my calendar and allowed me to claw out hours to write, *Sanibonani*.

To my Mount Zion movement, for the space to practice justice preaching and cultivate a community of reparative intercessors, *Sanibonani*.

To the PLOT participants, whose stories help to make my theory and practice sing, *Sanibonani*.

INTRODUCTION

Why We Are Lulled to Racial Inaction

Every time I laid my newborn son down for bed, a white-noise machine built into his bassinet soothed him to sleep. The sleep-aid device drowned out the noise of his mother recording dance tutorial videos for her website and his sibling dog, Wesley, barking at the front door, with nothing but the busy beats of the bustling Harlem streets on the other side. The machine distracted him from the loud realities that made up his fragile, rapidly changing world. It mimicked an environment he once knew—the womb. It simulated the familiar and comfortable to calm him as life moved forward with him blissfully unaware. The noise weighted his eyes into incessantly rapid blinking. I depended on white noise to still him to sleep as I strategized about how to use the silence to meet my to-do list.

A more insidious white noise distracts us into perpetual sleep meant to safeguard the status quo of racism. I categorize the racist ideas, speech, silence, and misrepresentations that protect and perpetuate Whiteness as white noise. When I discuss Whiteness in this book, I am not referring to skin color but rather to conscious or unconscious deference to unfounded notions of White superiority. White noise masks racial realities and allows persons, regardless of race, to ignore the call to disrupt systemic, structural, and individual racism. Though we dare not admit it, a majority of Americans adopt an eye-averted posture concerning race in our societies. White racist ideas, speech, and inaction exist across all racial lines due to how American public life shapes persons and perspectives. The omni-audible nature of Whiteness negates organic Black joy, peace, equality, love, and power, leaving images of Black violence, struggle, indignity, and destructibility seared into our public imagination.

White noise keeps us dismally unaware in a racialized world that marks life outcomes and templates of belonging according to the meaning invested in the color of skin. It provides cheap passes and comfortable distractions from the messes we have inherited and the others we have created. It keeps us in a moral infancy, stunting our growth as people poised to abolish racism. White noise condemns us to naivete, helplessness, and immaturity but without the innocence that typically accompanies these traits.

White noise encompasses much more than what we say or refrain from saying about our nation's founding ethical-spiritual dilemma, which continues to scar our souls. Coming to terms with our racist continuum means accepting that racist ideas produce racist policy and practices, and that racist policy and practices produce racist ideas. White noise fashions us into certain types of actors in the world. Our behaviors, attitudes, policies, institutions, and relationships are remarkably affected by white noise's impact on individuals and communities. These racialized sounds—discursive power—stipulate how we act and stall on questions of race, just as our actions and inactions communicate white noise. Even when we are unaware and not ill-intentioned, our conduct speaks a racial grammar of complicity or contestation.

Everything around us tells us to avoid the destabilizing despair behind race talk and racial justice advocacy as we sleepwalk toward destruction. As a nation and as individuals, we suffer from what

Walter Earl Fluker calls "social-political narcolepsy—a condition of uncontrollable sleeping."[1] So much of what we take in deadens our moral imagination and renders us deaf to the struggle for racial equity and repair. We all hear white noise differently, as it sends contradictory messages. It tells some that racism does not exist, others that racism exists but is not solvable. White noise convinces us to define White supremacy as police-involved killings of unarmed Black people; hooded marches through the old South, bolstered by the advocacy of White Citizens' Councils; or MAGA insurrections at the US Capitol—an already shaky civic temple of global democratic power.

However, racism is broader and more insidious than these events. We mistakenly identify racism as only brazen discrimination and physical violence. To protect ourselves, it is convenient to treat White supremacy as an anomaly unrelated to the specific social perils of today or as chauvinist attitudes that exist in the minds of extreme individuals. Racism is also the theological, historical, ideological, cultural, structural, and interpersonal practices that advantage one race group and disadvantage other groups as a result of race and skin color—which creates and perpetuates mass disparities. The white noise sounding from our televisions and textbooks, pulpits and corner offices, city halls and congressional chambers masks the truth about racism and quiets us into hibernation when humanity needs us awake and attentive.

White noise denies us a chance to live alert and conscious—to embrace a revolutionary realism—because we refuse to release the illusions of exceptionalism and greatness we harbor and advance when we cherry-pick from history. White noise protects us from the class-based racial nightmare in the United States, which started in the colonial context of stealing Native Americans' land and Black Africans for labor. White noise persuades Americans that we are all the Christopher Columbuses of the world, free to expand our particular values and innocently discover "new places" for that expansion. Our national fables coax us into identifying with the

Columbuses, Winthrops, Washingtons, and Adamses as one nation under God. We forget that so many of us better reflect the experiences of the Native people condemned to the treachery of disease and disinheritance. In the comfortable cribs of these illusions, we elect to spotlight the diplomatic genius of a slaveholding rapist like Thomas Jefferson, ignoring the carnage that slavery exacted due to his political hypocrisy concerning the equality of "all men."

This hazardous slumber facilitates silence on both sides of Whiteness as we live in its shadow of death. The inability to converse about race lulls both non-White and White people into an escapist sleep. White noise cancels out Black pain and the truth of America's history of racial terror, allowing us, like my infant son, to sleep through this moment in history, which is so ripe for a sincere racial reckoning.

The word *noise* derives from the Latin word for *nausea*—a feeling of uneasiness accompanied by the urge to vomit. In a sense, we move from offices to theaters to sanctuaries to bedrooms motion sick, vomiting up tragic—and potentially fatal—untruths about Black and Latinx communities. Unaware of their origins, we spew the ideas and sounds we hear. White noise sounds all around us and sometimes falls from our lips in statements such as these:

- "Black people are as equally racist as White people."
- "White people experience reverse discrimination."
- "America is a post-racial society."
- "If the Jews can make it, how come the Blacks can't?"
- "But my family never owned slaves."
- "I am not a racist; I voted for Obama."
- "I just want the most qualified person to get the job."
- "This is why we [Black people] can't have nice things."
- "She's so ghetto."
- "That's a hood dude."

- "How are you going to get a job with a name like that?"
- "He acts White."
- "You're not like other Black people."
- "It's not safe there."
- "Where are you really from?"

They all sound so innocent in the moment. The racialized habits—namely, in speech and silence—are the vomit of a subconscious governed by White fear and superiority. On a daily basis, we spew what we consume and experience without asking how we formed such opinions and feelings for ourselves and others.

My preaching ministry commenced at First Union Baptist Church in Galveston, Texas, one of the oldest independent Black churches in the state. I have many fond memories about that community of faith, which was wildly formative for my childhood and early conceptions of extended family. My maternal grandmother, Memi, sacrificed for and served this congregation until she died in July 2017, joining the realm of the ancestors. On many days, the most soaring memories of my grandmother's dignity have First Union as their setting. As a seventeen-year-old preacher, I delivered many sermons from First Union's pulpit, with my papa in the front row with the deacons and my grandmother at her usher post in the rear. In hindsight, my courage as a public speaker and intellectual crystalized behind that "sacred desk," with an affirming congregation of predominately elderly Black women and my grandparents occupying their respective seats of service and power.

All these positive recollections notwithstanding, one memory generates great horror and regret within me. After a rash of gun violence in a local public housing development, I took to the pulpit under the impression that our Black church fancied a sermon that addressed said violence. Ignorant of the statistics confirming the intraracial nature of most violence, I spent part of that sermon railing against gun violence in Black communities as something unique to Black communities. Under the guise of religion and a commitment to Black lives, I lifted the racist theme of "Black-on-Black crime." Dressed in an oversized blue suit and suspenders, I roared, "We need to pull up our pants, finish school, and put the guns down if we want to protect Black communities." The boy preacher in me responded to Black hopelessness and White supremacy manifested in intraracial gun violence by preaching the white noise I had consumed. To the cheers of Black congregants, I pathologized Blackness as inherently violent. I still remember feeling emboldened by the two ministers seated directly behind me and the two sections of the sanctuary choir that flanked the pulpit.

I had internalized the idea that "those Black men" typified what was wrong with Black communities and vomited it out on a Sunday morning as the Good News. There was no need for a White person to spread notions that stereotyped and dehumanized Black people that day. My church family needed only to listen to my racist proclamations, detached from any command of how concentrated poverty, racial isolation, and anti-Black ideas operate.

I communicated white noise in Black voice and Black sacred space because I trusted the myopic data my White social studies teacher taught. The detached numbers I had consumed confirmed the biases I formed in my middle-class cocoon. I normalized one of Hollywood's caricatures as if it cast the truest representation of "those Black people"—Black men and boys trapped in airtight pockets of poverty. Films like *Juice* (1992) and *Boyz n the Hood* (1991), pictures I once said petrified me more than any movie with Freddy Krueger or Michael Myers, stained my worldview and preaching. I consumed and communicated white noise with incalculable consequences for my audience. I was sleepwalking in racism.

Silence Is What Silence Does

The white noise of racism disguises the real, moving realities that we live—in boardrooms and classrooms, in Harvard Square and Times Square, on Facebook and at southern border walls. The sounds of kumbaya invitations, colorblind assertions, and vehement denials of racism only make the silence louder and our tone deafness decisively more aggressive. White noise drowns out the truth with lies about race, particularly when White privilege and power confront us and our tongues cling to the roofs of our mouths. When we believe that our silence about racism is safe, that there is no danger in avoiding racial situations, that racial justice is inevitable or impossible, we are practicing white noise.

Certain forms of silence are just as violent as the crack of the slaveholder's whip and the auction block. Parker Palmer purports, "We misunderstand nonviolence because we misunderstand violence, which goes well beyond the physical savagery that gets all the press. More common by far are those assaults on the human spirit so endemic to our time that we may not recognize them for the violent acts that they are."[2] Silence is cowardice that punctures the spirit.

Silence serves White privilege and threatens non-White survival. I will later argue that White privilege fails to ultimately benefit White people. But the idea of going through the day with little to no consideration of one's skin color remains foreign to non-White people. Regarding one's self outside racial identifiers is a privilege the majority of White people enjoy. This privilege cedes White people a freedom to ignore Black pain as isolated, individualized, and infrequent because it often transpires outside of White sight. Racism inheres a type of social distancing—long before COVID-19—in which most White people do not know Black people other than persons in their narrow circles or domestic service roles. In fact, the Public Religion Research Institute discovered that 75 percent of White people have no Black friends.[3] White people can watch eight minutes and forty-six seconds of Black death and dying—the murder of George Floyd—and easily return to life as usual, while some of us must carry a tragic question into many tomorrows: "Am I next?"

Silence also sometimes helps Black people survive. Many Black people maintain silence to prevent being labeled angry, hypersensitive, and irrational. Black people swallow outrage and offense at daily injustices to avoid jeopardizing their livelihood, to maintain equilibrium, and to protect themselves. The words of Zora Neale Hurston come to mind: "If you are silent about your pain, they'll kill you and say you enjoyed it."[4] This silence, too, betrays the ends of justice, crushing the respective, though related, promises of the *imago Dei*, abolition, and democracy.

So far, I have articulated a morally empty silence that advances corrosive self-interest or apathy toward racial inequality. However, not all silence is created equal. There is a difference between *deafening silence* and *disruptive silence*. In fact, some practices of silence, depending on their intent, add weight to the work of racial justice. We must ask, "What is my silence doing?" Is it exposing and contesting the dangers of white noise and Whiteness? Or is it white noise?

Deafening silence consents to the way things are due to disinterest in change. Deafening silence goes along to get along. Disruptive silence, however, contributes to racial repair through withdrawal and nonverbal participation by privileged communities. When practiced as a conspiracy of hope, silence can be seen as resistance, particularly when certain voices remain overrepresented in a given power game and those voices harbor potential for racial harm. The ceded, unearned credibility and authority of White people's voices, especially of White men, beg for circumstances to change when those voices yield to Black and Latinx participation and leadership. Disruptive silence materializes when a White person decides to make abundant space for Black voices and experiences in decision-making. The yielding of time typically dedicated to White people's voices disrupts the norms and draws attention to practices that silence non-White voices. Silence is disruptive when it dramatizes a refusal to participate in the status quo.

I recently came to terms with the power of disruptive silence. In 2017 I met with Cristian Moreno, a young immigration activist, to discuss plans for an Atlantic City demonstration, "A Day Without Immigrants." Demonstrations from Seattle to Maine criticized President Donald J. Trump's pledge to build a wall on the southern border between the United States and Mexico and the mass deportation of law-abiding Brown husbands and friends. Moreno resolved that this was a chance to uncover the xenophobic theatrics occurring in our backyard as we blinked our way into believing that New Jersey and Atlantic County could resist Trump-era deportation policies. The dreadfulness of our anti-Black and anti-Latinx immigration policies and practices only compounded with the countless number of US citizens racially profiled as undocumented and non-American. Moreno's demonstration bade immigrants of all nationalities to refuse to go to work, spend money, or attend school for one day in February.

Whether my closet risk-aversion or cynicism jaded my thinking, I remember inquiring, "What happens if the casinos fire them? Won't students be penalized for missing school? What if this triggers attention from ICE?" I went on and on with questions of caution. Moreno implored, "But, Pastor, justice is risky. The reality of our absence and silence will show them how important we are and what we deserve as people." I failed to see the power of disruptive silence beyond its risks.

Reparative Intercession: All Is Not Lost

The shelf life of racism depends on whether we can be honest about it. Many Americans of faith, specifically White Christians, reject their complicity in racism and claim to be nonracists. However, nonracist is not a real ethical orientation. We are either racist or anti-racism; there is no neutral, passive third way. Ibram X. Kendi asserts, "The opposite of a 'racist' isn't not racist. It is 'antiracist.' What's the difference? . . . One either allows racial inequities to persevere, as a racist, or confronts racial inequities, as an antiracist. There is no in-between safe space of 'not racist.' The claim of 'not racist' neutrality is a mask for racism."[5] By contrast, anti-racists intentionally advocate for policies and practices that guarantee racial equity, driven by a conviction of inherent racial equality. People of faith and conscience either disrupt racism as anti-racists or uphold racism as racists. Anti-racists intentionally confront racism—institutional and individual—with racial equity and repair as a way of life.

The stories, criticism, and practices in this book invite us into what I call *reparative intercession*. To be reparative intercessors is to take up oral, attitudinal, and behavioral practices that turn off the white noise and build the moral muscle to topple Whiteness. Drawing on the model of intercessory prayer, reparative intercession is public speech and action using one's power to benefit unrepresented and silenced individuals and communities. By attending to structural realities that blot out the power of non-White people, reparative intercession deviates from the platitudinous invitations to embrace human sameness and create interracial kumbaya experiences.

Reparative intercessors migrate through the world honoring the dignity of difference and leveraging their social privilege— maleness, Whiteness, middle- or upper-classness, US citizenship, Christian identity, or heterosexuality—to champion justice and equal opportunity for racialized others, people disadvantaged because of skin color, those whom Howard Thurman has said live with their backs against the wall.[6] For Christians, reparative intercession embodies a commitment to the way of Jesus of Palestine, combatting racist perspectives, policies, and practices as a cost of discipleship. For me, the love ethic of Jesus normalizes practicing socially conscious solidarity with humans assaulted by power structures and trapped under the suffocating knees of disinheritance and injustice.

The duty to stand in what Palmer terms "a tragic gap" draws us out of our neutrality or allegiance to racism. In *A Hidden Whole-*

ness, Parker claims, "The insight at the heart of nonviolence is that we live in a tragic gap—a gap between the way things are and the way we know they might be."[7] This tragic gap symbolizes the excruciating distance between the hard realities around us and what we know is possible—"not because we wish it were so, but because we've seen it with our own eyes."[8] White noise reinforces the racial power gap. Standing in the tragic gap means that the reparative intercessor learns to hold the tension between "reality and possibility" authentically and resiliently. This starts with a broad form of truth-telling that is noncooperative with how things are and a sacred imagination to see an alternative.

Say What? Racial Truth-Telling

In what follows, I propose reparative intercession as the bedrock of racial truth-telling. Here, my intellectual brother and education justice co-conspirator, Robert Harvey, reminds me of a helpful concept from one of our favorite thinkers, philosopher Michel Foucault. It's the concept of parrhesia. Most texts translate the Greek word *parrhesia* as "free speech." However, Foucault defines parrhesia as truth-telling for the benefit of others and oneself.

Too often the principle of free speech smoothly aids chauvinists who use the First Amendment to disgorge hate like bile. As I shrink from making a constitutional argument here, I settle on a concept of parrhesia as freedom and duty to speak truth to build and share power. Foucault offers:

> Parrhesia is a kind of verbal activity where the speaker has a specific relation to truth through frankness, a certain relationship to his own life through danger, a certain type of relation to himself or other people through criticism (self-criticism or criticism of other people), and a specific relation to moral law through freedom and duty. More precisely, parrhesia is a verbal activity in which a speaker expresses his personal relationship to truth, and risks his

life because he recognizes truth-telling as a duty to improve or help other people (as well as himself). In parrhesia, the speaker uses his freedom and chooses frankness instead of persuasion, truth instead of falsehood or silence, the risk of death instead of life and security, criticism instead of flattery, and moral duty instead of self-interest and moral apathy.[9]

Looking past Foucault's gender-biased language here, we need parrhesia in order to heal our hearts and society. The one who practices racial truth-telling affects others by sharing "as directly as possible what he actually believes."[10] Racial truth-telling assumes the speaking person owns their words and intends for those words to re-create the worlds we inhabit. Without a readiness to own the consequences of our words, truth-telling bounces across space and time absent of its most essential qualifier, a relationship with truth. Reparative intercession as racial parrhesia elects a dutiful path of frank, risk-inclined, critical truth-telling.

We significantly dial down white noise by reaching for a higher octave of engagement: honest, consistent, collective speech. We need a language for human belonging that snatches the veil off the lie that is race. Racism props itself up on the lie that race is biological and carries inherent meaning. Police brutality, education inequity, and the race-gender wealth gap make clear that we're long overdue for massive truth-telling concerning race, the omnipresence of racism in US history and institutions, and the ways each community bears responsibility for curating tomorrow.

Racism threatens to suck the air out of any room where we gather as a community, nation, and as individuals. No sphere of influence and concern legitimates any breathing room for our cowardice, ambivalence, and apathy. The various spaces we occupy for employment, leisure, or worship present a daunting incumbency to disrupt racism and silence white noise. Foucault proposes three domains where parrhesia should be practiced: small groups, the public, and the individual. By small groups, he means a defined community. Foucault contrasts small groups with "the public" as the institutions, spaces, and systems that order a society and wherein we carry out life. Respectively, community life, the public square, and personal relationships among individuals turn toward justice only when we speak hard truths about power and privilege.

The integrity of this work cannot be externally enforced. A person does this work because they feel a duty to do so. We speak reparatively, consciously, courageously, and introspectively about race as a spiritual imperative. The reparative intercessor accepts the risks of telling the truth in the name of human decency and non-White progression. Cheap racial progress rarely ignites backlash because it costs so little. Likewise, truth-telling associated with frugal courage lacks the character to be called racial parrhesia or reparative intercession. Black and other non-White lives matter to us when we speak up in ways that challenge our security and comfort. We cannot permit the better parts of our humanity to continue on unnourished and undeveloped "in the security of a life where the truth goes unspoken."[11] The promise of America and, more importantly, the *imago Dei* of our humanity obligate us to use our freedom in service of racial repair.

Reparative intercession reverberates as a counternarrative to the white noise that identifies the present world with ideas of societal fairness, racial progress, meritocracy, and colorblindness. Antiracist educator Derald Wing Sue writes, "The counter-narratives of race talk are extremely threatening to Whites and to our society because they may unmask the secrets of power and privilege, and how the public transcript of a master narrative justifies the continued subordination of people of color."[12] Our shared future depends on the back talk of reparative intercession, which challenges historical and present racial tribulations that harm non-White communities and individuals.

As we will explore, silencing white noise means accepting everyday consequences. One must be ready to lose a job or promotion when standing up to a supervisor or a treasured relationship when challenging a friend or family member. In some cases, one must find the inner resolve to sacrifice political favor by refusing to allow a public servant to proceed without apology for their comments and voting record. In rare but not impossible circumstances, racial truth-telling even robs some of the guarantees of safety when their voices expose and compromise the power and privilege of the few.

Appeals to racial equity never come without costs for reparative intercessors. Reparative intercession involves status-threatening conversations, starting with the self, that will lead to honest interpersonal dialogue and public engagement. What makes the truth risk-responsive is that it "comes from 'below' as it were, and is directed towards 'above.'"[13] Racial truth-telling requires the bold willingness to unsettle actors who hold some level of social privilege and power—namely, the capacity to retaliate. This is mundane, on-the-ground, bottom-up power. Again, while this is a classic summons to speak "truth to power," this is a call to speak truth to build and share power over and over and over.

In fall of 2015, I was part of a panel forum exploring the history and future of progressive faith communities at the intersections of gender, mass incarceration, and sexuality. During the question-and-answer time, a White attendee approached the microphone: "Rev. Francois, thank you for your talk. You rightly identified the insanity of racism in our criminal justice system." I nodded in anticipation of a question that might lead us toward practical approaches to confront mass incarceration. "You are preaching to the choir here. This is a message those other White people need to hear." This person, and most certainly other attendees, viewed the two-hour discussion on dismantling racism as an event for other White people—the real racists. The constant hum that racism is someone else's responsibility allowed the participant to deny any personal accountability.

I responded, "Well, even the choir needs continuous rehearsal."

Casting out White supremacy requires daily intentionality and vigor. No one ages or reads their way out of racism. In fact, no one is a member of the choir of anti-racism; we all exist in the congregation of the hopeful—people perpetually on the verge of ousting our next demons. If we are to assume the mantle of practitioners of hope, then we need continuing education in the art of racial truth-telling and repair to end the everyday events that prevent us from inhabiting a world in which Whiteness comes undone for good.

First Things First: Reconciliation Pipe Dreams

Reparative intercession is not a call to racial reconciliation. James Cone, the progenitor of Black liberation theology, pierced the bubble of optimism by asking, "Reconciled to what?"[14] We must repair before we can reconcile. Without repairing the harm—psychological and physical—racial reconciliation rings hollow. The desire for universal brotherhood and sisterhood that avoids treating past and present racism is a function of white noise. The future of humanity asks us to abandon our assumptions that "togetherness" is a cure-all for generations of anti-Black exclusion, violence, economics, politics, and religion.

Likewise, reparative intercession goes beyond merely celebrating cosmetic diversity. The abolition of racial segregation and inequality mandate a form of speech—and ultimately practice—interested in building and sharing power with those condemned as "the wretched of the earth." We need a new foundational question to silence white noise en route to upending racism. A diversity approach asks, "Who is present?" An inclusion lens asks, "Who is participating?" A call to reparative intercession asks, "Who has power?" Justice and repair account for the differences in needs, privileges, opportunities, and burdens in pursuit of authentic human equality. This work is about power-building and power-sharing.

We must refuse the diversity facade in favor of power-sharing and repair first. "The Whiteness problem" necessitates more than appeals for unity and hopes for "not seeing color." Racial repair is a process that accounts for and addresses the harm caused by racism. It leads to racial justice, and social, political, and economic equality regardless of race. Racial repair and racial justice are preludes to racial reconciliation. Racial justice paves the way for racial reconciliation. Without abolition and repair, racial reconciliation floats in the air as an empty, intangible figment of the White imagination and a sedative deception of white noise. Before we can live in harmony and oneness, we must pursue uncomfortable race-related conversations and actions that lead to repairing the harm inflicted by racism over the past four centuries. The unity for which we long remains a farce if we retreat from the heart-convicting, emotionally tiring, soul-freeing work of reparative intercession.

In *Dear White Christians: For Those Still Longing for Racial Reconciliation*, Jennifer Harvey fuels my sense of a reparative framework for racial justice. As a self-identified *prophetic* White evangelical, Harvey uses her social location to mine the pitfalls and potentials of White evangelicalism and Whiteness in America as political ideology, religious identity, and White privilege. Harvey examines a history of mainline Protestant commitments to the question of racial justice. She distinguishes between center-left White Christians and White evangelicals—the former being committed to racial reconciliation devoid of racial equity, the latter rejecting the existence of structural racism altogether. In short, mainline White Protestants acknowledge the existence of structural racism but tend to place a premium on reconciliation and multiracial community-formation, not thoroughgoing racial equity and reparative justice.

Diversity remains an ideal in Christian communities of various ideological shapes and racial compositions. But for numerous houses of worship, this amounts to a short-sighted, shallow goal that gratifies personal preferences instead of forming authentic strategies to undo the racism that corrodes public life beyond our sanctuaries. Racial reconciliation prioritizes the abstract notion of "human oneness" without addressing the social messes spawned by White terrorism—a terrorism regularly baptized by Christian doctrine and practice—which creates the need for reconciliation in the first place. This inexpedient collective call for reconciliation allows us to focus on racial and ethnic differences without assessing how historical, material, and structural conditions give meaning to those distinctions. Through reconciliation, we further cling to our illusions of innocence.

This highlights a failure of our "reconciliation fantasies." A reconciliation approach to our racial history flattens the very difference it claims to want to achieve in our sanctuaries. Though I can, and will later, make a reparative case for human oneness, the escapist and reductionist language about human sameness addressed here obscure each group's unique experiences in the United States and their relationships to White supremacy. Harvey and Cone dared me to ask some questions about the reconciliation paradigm: (1) To what are we being reconciled? (2) Do we honor our differences, our sameness, or both as God-given? and (3) What does reconciliation cost the powerful and the vulnerable?

Due to white noise, many of us undertake reconciliation without first interrogating the meaning, assumptions, histories, and privileges of Whiteness. Reconciliation does not cost the powerful and privileged anything that alters the ways they show up in the world. Whiteness compromises the hope for true reconciliation when it hinges on the insinuation that Black people, and all non-White people violated by racism, should just trust White people "again" without White people qualitatively and quantitively transforming anything real.

Harvey writes, "In few to no situations of harm and violence, do we expect a victimized party to move to trust until there is evidence that the victimizer will unequivocally cease to victimize and thoroughly repent."[15] The kumbaya dream that race and the past do not matter—an expression of white noise—permits White people to experience the warm fuzzies. They pat themselves on the back while receiving higher wages, inherited resources, biased credit scores, and other unearned advantages. The unaddressed power and privilege still worsen the opportunities of the Black and Latinx people to whom they claim to be reconciled. Our pining for reconciliation speaks to our infantile imagination, telling us daily that the past is in the past and that the future is a cheap manipulation of the present racial dread we have so long wanted to merely disappear.

Drawing on Harvey's work, reparative intercession (1) recognizes racism as a social construct with material and discursive histories that impact personal and communal life differently depending on which side of White supremacy one lives, (2) accepts there is no universal lived experience in the United States, and (3) invests in practices that disrupt and repair the harm.[16] Harvey purports, "If concrete, material structures created race and continue to give race the lion's share of its actual meaning, taking history seriously makes it impossible to avoid speaking about perpetrators and victims, about the persons who benefitted and continue to benefit unjustly from these legacies, and about the persons who were and continue to be harmed."[17] When we confront the power and privilege baked into our communities and institutions, we will owe something. Reparative intercession involves a healthy fusion of speech and action—parrhesia and showing up—under the impetus of racial repair.

Finding Our Rhythm

There is a rhythmic art to race talk and anti-racist action that initiates racial repair. I call these principled practices "rhythms" because reparative intercession rearranges our lives through disciplined, artistic, and recurrent explorations of new languages, relationships, emotions, thinking, activities, and challenges. In music, a rhythm is an ordered arrangement of elements that moves a sound forward. Reparative intercession creates new sounds that replace the white noise shaping our values, convictions, appetites, and behaviors. Rhythm is the foundation for all elements of musical movement; it connotes an artistic enterprise. Reparative intercession is an art, not a science. It is not a standardized set of rules that straitjacket human interaction. The work of the Underground Railroad, an American campaign to end chattel slavery—the nation's deepest racial and economic injustice—was guided by rhythmic moans, groans, songs, and coordination.

Replacing white noise with the rhythms of reparative intercession is part of dismantling White supremacy. Each succeeding chapter of this book identifies a feature of white noise and highlights one of the rhythms of reparative intercession that serves as a corrective. These rhythms invite us to become and build communities of reparative intercessors—people who dare to repair the harm of racism by faithfully speaking up and acting up on behalf of the unprotected, invisible, and disempowered when it comes to race. Each rhythm leads to various practices and perspectives to silence the white noise around us and within us.

The six rhythms of reparative intercession are:

1. Cues to color: embracing difference as gift
2. Momentum to encounter: confronting the histories of Whiteness
3. Pattern recognition: honoring our interdependence
4. Syncopated identity: exploring our fuller selves
5. Pulse to risk: sacrificing our power and privilege
6. Downbeat truth: naming our complicity in racism

Chapter 1 explores how the *cues to color* honor the ways racial uniqueness adds texture to the tapestry of human history and emerging possibilities. This rhythm replaces the white noise "I don't see color," acknowledging and embracing the divinity of difference as a gift to society. In chapter 2, we unpack the *momentum to encounter*, a rhythm challenging us to confront the histories of

Whiteness that shape our world. Confronting the past that is alive in the present rejects the white noise that allows us to feel that "It's not my fault. Slavery was so long ago. Get over it."

In chapter 3, we mine the strengths of *pattern recognition* as a rhythm of reparative intercession that quiets the white noise that compels us to say "I've had it hard too, but I worked hard." This way of knowing and being appreciates our interdependence and shared futures. Chapter 4 presents us with the opportunity to explore the fullness of our identities. Cultivating a *syncopated identity* allows us to own our racial identity and its numerous intersections and courageously pursue cross-racial contact instead of asking, "Why does everything have to be about race?" Chapter 5 turns down the white noise that "It's not my job to fix racism" with the *pulse to risk* our power and privilege as an act of holiness. We consider faith's response to the call to end interpersonal and institutional racisms as abolition spirituality. In chapter 6, we make room for *downbeat truth*, a rhythm that harvests the discomfort of telling on ourselves—naming our complicity in racism—so that we can set aside the excuse that "I'm scared of the backlash."

Reparative intercession prods questions like the following:

- Am I willing to pay a price? What am I willing to give up?
- Am I committed after the news cycle fades and the issue is no longer right in front of me?
- Do I see the sacredness of all non-White lives?
- Can I handle the backlash?
- Am I ready to confront my complicity and reimagine my responsibility?

While reparative intercession primarily forms new habits of advocating and showing up for the other, in a profound sense, it frees us from the material and audible forces of Whiteness that arrest and tell us who is valued, how to act, where it is safe, when to speak, and what to say. After a lifetime of anxiety, it remains possible to speak compassionately and intelligently when police kill another unarmed Black person like Breonna Taylor. You can be transparent about your implicit biases that crowd out your courage to post "Black Lives Matter" after someone on your Twitter feed writes, "Blue Lives Matter" or "All Lives Matter." With introspection, you can respond faithfully when matters of race arise. Reparative intercession allows people of faith and conscience to silence the white noise of racism and begin to redeem a new dream, not the founding fathers' dream, of America as a multiracial democracy rooted in political liberty, human equality, and economic sufficiency.

"I don't see color. We are all the same in Christ."

1

Cues to Color

Embracing Difference as Gift

I first encountered "colorblind Christianity" during my second year of seminary. En route to Cambridge, Massachusetts, from Charlotte, my seatmate on a flight appeared more interested in engaging me than I could muster the will to reciprocate. After preaching at a couple services for a congregation in the Charlotte area, I had pulled an all-nighter with Red Bull and Doritos to submit a midterm paper. Quite familiar with last-minute intensive writing, I still experienced acute levels of fatigue that morning, perhaps due to the turnaround commute from North Carolina to Massachusetts. I can still hear Dr. Jonathan Walton reprimanding me for accepting such engagements in my middle year of seminary, when he saw it as more prudent for me to be stationary and focused on my heavy course load.

While adding some final details to my footnotes, I pulled J. Kameron Carter's book *Race: A Theological Account* from my bag. My seatmate asked me about it. I explained Carter's attempt to trace dominant Christianity as a cultural product of the White Western world that informs how we understand race and see and move in the world. She probed, "Why would you read something like that? That's not the gospel of Christ." After I took a few more moments to explain the project, she said, "The gospel is not about race. It's colorless, raceless." Her passion might have proven persuadable if not for an image of a White Jesus embellishing a bookmark protruding from the top of her romance novel. She took issue with a book she assumed charged certain forms of Christianity as being allied with White supremacy. But her bookmark, too, made a claim about race and Christianity. White noise permitted her to claim a raceless gospel while holding on to a White Jesus. Colorblindness typically blurs every color but White (Whiteness, to be more precise).

Colorblind Christianity (1) denies the diversities of the image of God, (2) impairs a vocation to abolish racial injustices, (3) upholds the sin of Whiteness, (4) blames the racially unprotected for their social location, and (5) exaggerates racial progress. Anthea Butler, in *White Evangelical Racism*, writes, "This color-blind gospel is how evangelicals used the biblical scripture to affirm that everyone, no matter what race, is equal and that race does not matter. The reality of the term 'color-blind,' however, was more about making Black and other ethnic evangelicals conform to whiteness and accept white leadership as the norm both religiously and socially."[1] This adaptation of Christian religion is the curious offspring of colorblind racism.

Colorblind Christianity first signaled for me that we practice many "Christianities" in this nation. I often refer to Christianity in the plural to dramatize the various shades, theologies, liturgical expressions, and political priorities that exist under the moniker of "Christian." Christian religion is far from monolithic and manifests in distinct ways politically, morally, and doctrinally to the point of appearing incohesive and antithetical on major truth claims and practices. For instance, the Christian faith American slaves practiced in the brush harbors—beyond the supervision of plantation preachers—taught of a God and Jesus organically and irrevocably committed to abolition, which markedly departed from the slaveholding aims of the master class's Christian religion wedded to the maintenance of the chattel system. Their approaches to God functioned under the same name but could not be more different. Colorblind Christianity seeks to underrate the role race and racism played in America and its religions about Jesus. There is a penchant to disremember these distinct approaches to "the faith."

When white noise denies the existence of racism by touting colorblindness, we must practice the cues to color—a rhythm of reparative intercession that recognizes and embraces the divinity of difference as a gift to society. The cues to color—identifying the ways skin color matters socially, economically, religiously, and politically—start with attending to the function and meaning of race in the United States.

Colorblind Racism

Colorblindness uses an idea of our biological human sameness to overlook cultural and experiential differences and negate economic and political opportunities that differ due to race. To be colorblind is to deny the structure of society. White noise cues us to feign blindness to race and skin color and how they shape real life. This "covert" racism, whether associated with a religion or not, minimizes the historical longevity of racist social arrangements and engenders substitute reasons for the lack of social and economic parity between White and Black lives. It explains inequality using nonracial calculations. Colorblind racism promotes white noise in four ways, through the myths of (1) equal opportunism, (2) cultural assimilation, (3) social naturalism, and (4) naive romanticism.[2]

Equal opportunism peddles the assumption that there is un-inhibited access to jobs, housing markets, schools, and influence, and that each individual must own the responsibility of taking advantage of what America offers. I use opportun*ism* here to characterize this myth as a type of flawed belief system related to opportunity, which dictates how we engage institutions and interpret the life-outcomes of others. It is White privilege to live willfully seduced by the idea that all hardworking persons approach loan officers, human resource directors, or county prosecutors on level playing fields or even with the presumption of fairness in the process. A trope of this white noise is "Minorities should not get special consideration." One might reject programs like affirmative action on the basis of reverse discrimination against hardworking White people or unfair biases for undeserving non-White people. This approach clings to the promises of America and the values sacrificed for and championed by social struggles like abolition and the civil rights movement without accounting for the barriers faced by non-White people today. Here, impartiality moonlights as ignorance—erasing the past that makes a reparative consideration of race necessary in college admissions and employment. These ideas find a foothold in the myths of racial equality and meritocracy—an American fabrication that diligence and hard work will be rewarded regardless of race.

Cultural assimilation blames victims of discrimination for their social location due to behavioral and moral degeneracy. The assimilationist believes that a group can be bettered by adopting the culture of another group. Assimilation assumes one should discard one's own culture and institutions for those of the ruling class. This type of white noise communicates that minorities live trapped at the bottom due to strained family relations and a lack of motivation.

Some non-White people amplify this white noise when they assent to stereotypes about laziness, family dysfunction, hood culture, and the like. For example, cultural racism frames Black people as products of problematic social settings and poor personal choices without acknowledging structural and governmental practices designed to disinherit Black life. The trauma of self-blame surfaces when Black and Latinx persons rationalize their economic and employment distance from White people by saying things like, "I didn't go to the right schools. My historically Black college/university didn't prepare me to compete in White spaces."

Social naturalism sees racial isolation as a result of personal choice. Eduardo Bonilla-Silva posits, "The word 'natural' or the phrase 'that's the way it is' is often interjected to normalize events or actions that could otherwise be interpreted as racially motivated (residential segregation) or racist (preference for whites as friends and partners)."[3] Social naturalism is a frame of reference that doesn't account for the structures that prevent people from choosing where to live. Want and preference die in the face of redlining, racial covenants,[4] and economic thresholds. White noise explains concentrated poverty and racial exclusion as self-segregation.

Naive romanticism overstates racial progress and reduces racism to heinous and overt forms of discrimination—for example, a police-killing of an unarmed Black person, warehousing Latin American children in unsanitary cages, or the use of certain epithets. It insists that things are "so much better than they were." Colorblind racism minimizes contemporary injustices by measuring them against the experiences of previous generations. For instance, a person might reject anti-Black job discrimination—last hired but first fired—by comparing it to the Jim Crow job culture that criminalized multiracial workplaces. "But we've come a long way" attempts to invalidate the lived experiences of non-White people.

From my organizing experience, these forms of colorblind racism are often intertwined with each other. Racial equity in public education has dominated much of my community organizing over the last five years. In 2020, I engaged with a few school districts suffering from racial and economic segregation. In a Zoom consultation with leaders, questions about why school segregation exists emerged. A neighboring majority-White school district had filed a petition to the state to sever a one-hundred-year send-receive relationship with a majority-Black-and-Brown district. Due to the agreement, the White district was sending one hundred high school students to the non-White district each year. However, the White families consistently found alternatives to enrolling their students in the receiving school. Their petition intended to replace their de facto segregation with de jure segregation. White flight would leave the district 100 percent non-White.

We campaigned to resist this potential state-sponsored segregation. Though the leaders of the non-White district supported our grassroots campaign, they opted to abstain from the legal fight. In that Zoom meeting, one leader remarked, "Well, it is their choice where their kids are educated. People go to school where they live." Another retorted, "Y'all sound quite alarmist. You're talking about this like we live in the Jim Crow South. I don't blame them for wanting out. It's high time we get our act together as a people."

In an attempt to tell me why desegregation is not their fight, a school board member reiterated, "You really cannot tell people where to send their children to school. Parents decide where students live, which determines where they are schooled." He continued, "[Our district] is majority Latino and Black because we prefer to live with each other." These Black and Latinx district leaders saw family participation in their district and residency in their city as a choice. A false assumption about how power works sustained their white noise.

Equal opportunism, cultural assimilationism, social naturalism, and naive romanticism came together in one meeting. In a single setting, the school-district leaders blamed themselves and their constituents for inequality, evoked the myth of choice, and romanticized all the changes since Jim Crow. They merely blinked at the decades of forces that fixed residential arrangements in their town and the impacts of White and middle-class divestment and abandonment. White noise silenced the truth behind school segregation and amplified the presumption of this powerlessness as self-inflicted, a personal choice, and unlike what we experienced as a nation prior to the *Brown v. Board of Education* decision. Colorblind racism let Whiteness off the hook. And it force-fed the self-accusing reasons for non-White problems down non-White throats, which came right back up at that meeting.

It's Baked In

White noise tells us that systemic and structural racism exist only in the minds of others. At times it identifies racism only as brazen discrimination and violence; however, racial discrimination ranges from individual actions to institutional practices. Racism exists as hierarchy and subjugation, not simply as hatred and slurs. As I noted earlier in my framing of white noise, mass disparities along the lines of race stem from advantages doled out to one racial group and denied to another through theological, historical, ideological, cultural, structural, and interpersonal practices. As colorblindness, racism masterfully normalizes White power and privilege while simultaneously obscuring histories of anti-Black violence and mass racial inequities baked into the fabric of our institutions.

The Alt-Right, Ku Klux Klan, Proud Boys, and other neo-Nazi groups compose a lethal fringe element of the American body politic. Events like the January 6th Capitol insurrection in 2021, instigated by the then-sitting president of the United States, egged on by some members of Congress, and praised by some Christian talking heads, unveil the national necessity to resist and abolish White supremacy in all its terrorizing and morally anemic forms. Nonetheless, when we reduce White supremacy to tiki torches, burning crosses, and lynchings, or a man suffocating under the knee of a cop, we endorse the gross fictive innocence of our republic, which works to shield the expansiveness of racism. Structural violence must incite in us the same level of righteous indignation as brazen discrimination and violence. By no means an exhaustive list, omnipresent forms of White supremacy include underfunded urban schools, mass incarceration and Black criminalization born out of a government-manufactured war on drugs, redlining that created pockets of non-White poverty, a gendered and racialized wealth gap mirroring realities of the 1950s, hiring discrimination against the formerly incarcerated, and legalized voter suppression enabled by the Supreme Court's decision to pull the teeth out of the Voting Rights Act of 1965.

Reparative intercession requires more than denouncing hate groups and calling people out for racial slurs. The reach of Whiteness in our communities obligates us to name zero tolerance discipline policies in schools as racist. Poverty wages for Black women and Latinas are racist. Public policies that use identification requirements as cover for voter suppression are racist. School funding formulae largely based on segregated property taxes are racist.

A Doctrine of Whiteness

To be clear, race is a social construction loaded with meanings produced by a ruling class over hundreds of years, not a definitive biological category. Racial difference and definitions grew out of manipulations of science, biased notions of beauty, and the historical emergence of Europeans as exploiters of creation. The concept of Whiteness introduced at the beginning of this book clarified that it is bigger than skin color. Whiteness refers to a structural logic and a way of being and knowing, not simply skin color or ancestry. People willfully and unknowingly defer to the baseless notion of White superiority. White supremacy is a doctrine that governs our lives, forges ways of thinking, and produces frameworks for meaning. In a sense, white noise compels us to genuflect at the shrines of Whiteness. Whiteness silences and works against the legitimacy of non-White equality and belonging. I use "non-White" throughout this book instead of "persons of color" as a way of centering Whiteness as a moral crisis, theological heresy, and public hazard for all people.

In *Prophesy Deliverance!*, Cornel West tracks the emergence and logic of White racism in the modern West.[5] He builds on Foucault's genealogical approach to explain why White and Black people, irrespective of racial identity, cannot escape the grip of this power. Discursive power relates to the rules and fundamental assumptions that govern practices, self-identification, and social interactions of a subject's body (and mind). Whiteness is the noise, language, and doctrine of America. White racism persists as a subjectless form of power working beneath the consciousness of human subjects regardless of racial identity.[6] We all consume and communicate white noise because of the stealthy, omnipresent nature of Whiteness, which shapes us and works on us outside of our awareness.

Christian discourse and identity played a significant role in the European colonial project. The demarcation between "believer" and "unbeliever" was used to justify brutalities toward peoples of Africa and the Americas.[7] The barbarity mapped onto these darker bodies resulted in their being seen as "heathens." Religious superiority morphed into racial superiority over time. The doctrine of Whiteness entails the belief that White people enjoy (1) an exceptional ancestry that legitimates a right to dominate and control, (2) primary ownership of the meaning of humanity and Americanness, (3) a racial hierarchy that perceives the other as inherently dangerous and inferior, (4) mythic social innocence regarding America's racial tragedy, and (5) systemic and structural advantages due utterly to skin color.

Whiteness is systemic and structural sin—a condition of being, seeing, and knowing that threatens the integrity of creation in general and humanity in particular. Whiteness is sin, not an identity, that is ours to purge from the world. Three metaphors for the sin of Whiteness emerge: it is idolatrous, demonic, and segregationist.

White Sin: Idolatry

Whiteness endures as a sin because it assumes the role of a god in society. Whiteness is an idolatrous religious tradition in the

United States marked by its own deity, public and private rituals, and symbols. Omnipresence is an attribution typically reserved for a god, but it applies here because racism is all around us— entrenched within the diverse peoples and structures of America. In 1965, theologian George Kelsey wrote, "Racism as a faith is a form of idolatry, for it elevates a human factor to the level of the ultimate. The god of racism is the race, the ultimate center of value. . . . For the racist, race is the final point of reference for decision and action, the foundation upon which he organizes his private life, public institutions and public policy, and even his religious institutions."[8] The dangerous, life-foreclosing deity of Whiteness dislocates the person from God, creation, and the self, which I later unpack as the sin of segregation. The god of Whiteness bids us to do the dirty work, the iniquitous labor of covertly and deliberately enforcing a hierarchy of lives according to the doctrinal rules of race.

Whiteness persists as an American god—what Paul Tillich would call an "Ultimate Concern"[9]—with altars in every American school, police station, courthouse, bank, and legislative hall. An ultimate concern, in practice, becomes a person's god. Our ultimate concern utterly grasps us with the power to destroy or heal us. Nationalism lifts the nation to the status of the ultimate. Sexism concerns itself with male power. Capitalism is ultimately consumed with production, profits, and class locations. Comparably, racism venerates Whiteness as the ultimate concern. Whiteness grounds the being of people who are psychologically and materially privileged, protected, and produced by a racist nation. Therefore, we surrender to Whiteness as a false god occupying our ideals, relationships, and souls.

Racism—a civic religious system—creates God in the image of Whiteness. Any deity fashioned out of the raw material of humanity's social insecurity, exclusivist supremacy, or quest for power amounts to a false god. Whiteness as an idol, a symbol created in the image of its worshipers, profanes the ultimacy and freedom of the God of love. "Idolatry is the elevation of a preliminary concern to ultimacy. Something essentially conditioned is taken as unconditional, something essentially partial is boosted into universality, and something essentially finite is given infinite significance."[10] Racism projects values, characteristics, and the insecurities of White supremacy onto the divine, compromising the confessed eternality and ultimacy of its conception of God. Tragically, the idol of Whiteness marches in lockstep with many forms of Christian religion. It is hard not to become White Christian polytheists even with Black and other non-White skin because the chaplains of privilege and priests of inequality sell us the promise that we can be white as snow.

This allusion to the ultimacy of Whiteness in America underscores the heretical notion of White supremacy, which is often thinly veiled under the bloodstained banner of a Christian religion. However, the banner of this Christian religion is not stained by the blood of Jesus but by the blood of innumerable Black, Native, Asian, and Latinx bodies. Our prayers to the God who created us fail to discontinue our service as acolytes to the god of Whiteness we cling to as an idol.

White Sin: Demonic

Whiteness denies the humanity of the other, which renders it a sin. It is demonic. The tragic character of Whiteness casts non-White, particularly Black, personhood as a threatening "thing." Whiteness hinges on the condemnation of non-White people. The growing cultural and social insecurity of Whiteness enfleshes itself as racial narcissism and racist paranoia. White power thrives on the negation of Black power, Latinx power, or Asian power. Tillich writes, "Power is real only in its actualization, in the encounter with other bearers of power and in the ever-changing balance which is the result of these encounters."[11] Illegitimate power entails the projection of an image of "the enemy" that has nothing to do with reality. Said image reveals a demonic-destructive function in persons and groups responsible for producing it. White privilege at the expense of the equality and dignity of non-White persons renders White supremacy demonic and an illegitimate form of power to be contested and countered.

White noise impacts our national gaze. Due to white noise, the American gaze affirms negative assumptions and stereotypes of non-White bodies. The Western world venerates Whiteness and devalues the other—namely, Blackness—as some*thing* to be managed and rejected. Shaped by the normative gaze, America maintains White culture as the ideal through political and religious practices, and all other cultures represent degenerations from the standard of Whiteness.[12]

By demonic, I mean any power that impairs human flourishing, autonomy, and creativity. The dehumanization of any class of people is demonic. In a society governed by Whiteness, the non-White person emerges from the social insecurity of Whiteness as the enemy of the public. America's regime of violence denies that non-White people are rights-bearing persons. No remorse is shown for punishing, marginalizing, and annihilating the subhuman other. *Thingification* is the process of mapping attributes of danger, guiltiness, and criminality on human bodies. It amounts to demonizing and dehumanizing a group or person. Likewise, the thingification of Blackness, in political-theological terms, is the creation of an enemy, a scapegoat, an other. This demonization and depersonalization of the other strips the person or group of its autonomy, "its spontaneity, of its living response."[13] Racism tracks onward as a divisive, dehumanizing form of power, denying non-White beauty, freedom, life, love, and creativity.

White Sin: Segregation

Whiteness promotes the politics and dogmatics of separation. Sin does not merely separate us from God and others; the separation itself is the sin. Tillich conceives, "To be in the state of sin is to be in the state of separation. And separation is threefold: there is separation among individual lives, separation of a man from himself, and separation of all men from the Ground of Being [Tillich's proxy for God]."[14] Whiteness detaches us from our origin, self, and others, giving tragic meaning to racial group relations and lived experiences. The estrangement is a gap between the way things should be and the way things are, particularly for those on the upper side of political and economic power. Sin creates the tragic gaps reparative intercessors must occupy to abolish racism and repair its generational harms. Whiteness estranges a person from the gift of living in community, with the capacity to connect with oneself, others, and the divine. White supremacy is a form of self-exile from one's humanity, God, and other human beings.

Again, sin does not merely separate us from God and one another; the separation is itself the sin. Jim Crow era segregation was a period of forced racial separation in American history, marked by lynchings and preceded by chattel slavery. It offers a chilling symbol for White sin as separation and estrangement. Kelsey calls segregation "the principal plan of political action of racist faith."[15] He adds, "From a Christian viewpoint, segregation not only denies the God-given dignity of man, it also violates the human oneness which God the Creator established. [Humanity] is created for community. From the hand of God, [the human] is for [the human]. [The human] is the covenant-partner of God and [humanity]."[16] Diminishing the value and life of the other and banishing them to a proscribed location are inherent to the sin of Whiteness.

The segregationist nature of Whiteness disconnects our souls from our bodies, forcing us to deny the beauty of our skin as non-White people and underwrites the deadly stigmatization and demonization of our differences. White lies breach our public trust, pushing communities apart based on the ruses of race. White lies are never little in terms of the impact they have on non-White lives. White lies turn public schools into prison preparatory academies instead of institutions of human enrichment. White lies deny voting rights to millions of non-White citizens returning from prison.

White lies allow police officers to kill unarmed Black men and go home with their guns, badges, and pensions. White lies allow a mayor to convince a city that we must throw teenagers against a wall and frisk them to fix crime. White lies disembody the historical Jesus, co-opting and converting him into a placid abstraction to support Christian Whiteness masquerading as evangelicalism.

The Souls of White Folks

Whiteness forcefully persists, whether or not White people consciously espouse racist ideas or practice anti-Black, anti-Latinx, or anti-Asian behaviors. Peggy McIntosh points out that "as a white person, I realized I had been taught about racism as something which puts others at a disadvantage, but had been taught not to see one of its corollary aspects, white privilege, which puts me at an advantage."[17] The indictment of White privilege insults many White people because they hear it as ignoring their hard work to secure the current circumstances of their lives. One White person I met at a conference shared, "I think of White privilege as the absence of certain things. I may have had a tight budget when I shopped, but I've never had a security guard following me. When I got pulled over for speeding once in my twenties, I did get a ticket, but I did not have to fear for my life during the traffic stop." However, White privilege ultimately fails to protect White humanity—the deep structure of the soul that makes us available to one another.

During the summer of 2020, I accepted an invitation to converse with two White evangelical pastors about race and racism for a multiracial virtual audience. The question of "White blessing versus White privilege" landed right in front of me. One of the ministers, a retired pastor and former public-school educator, rebuffed me for naming the norms of his life as unearned social privileges. "Willie, you call them privilege. I call them White blessings," he insisted. "I grew up with two parents who loved me. I was supported by gainfully employed family members. That's not White privilege. It's a blessing."

Beyond the obvious white noise of insinuating that Black families, as a rule, lack the basic structure he named, he obscured the structural realities his Whiteness permits him to avoid. His worldview gives no account for forces like over-policing and a punitive legal system that empties some Black households of wage-earning parents. He had not overtly considered how 246 years of unpaid labor and 90 years of Jim Crow poverty wages still impact "gainful employment" for Black families. His White blessings have meant curses visited on Black people. This spiritualized thinking about being blessed allows White people to scapegoat God for the systems that benefit them and shred Black life.

White privilege forecloses the vitality of *ubuntu*—what the late Archbishop Desmond Tutu defined as the moment when "'my humanity is caught up, is inextricably bound up, in yours.' We belong in a bundle of life. We say, 'A person is a person through other persons.'"[18] Any privilege derived at the expense of the dignity and future of "an other" costs a person their humanity. Unchecked, their privilege becomes their one-way ticket into a hell, where they may lift up their eyes only to be tormented daily by the onslaught of self-hatred. Privilege and supremacy destroy the soul; they make one "hideously empty,"[19] and turn people into "moral monsters."[20]

White Grief, Not (Just) White Guilt

The cues to color initiate the process of replacing White guilt with White grief. Reparative intercession starts with seeing differences as gifts of creation, which banishes implicit and explicit beliefs that one race is superior to another. You should allow yourself to feel the loss of letting go of Whiteness. How can we abolish racism and its corresponding disparities if we are dishonest and Pollyannish about what race means to public life? The cues to color are a form of intentional color-consciousness that acknowledges the divinity of difference without belittling the grotesque ways race serves as the chief indicator for how a person's life unfolds. Color-consciousness frees us to account for the massive impact race has on how we see people, where they work, education outcomes, life expectancy, and so forth. Disparities find compelling explanations in how the doctrine of Whiteness privileges some and marginalizes others. Therefore, color-consciousness unveils the extent to which Whiteness forecloses any chance to embrace the divinity of difference.

The fear of owning experiential differences and opportunity inequities related to race often leads to White guilt when we encounter ugly historical realities. In the context of racial oppression, guilt cracks open the door to healthy feelings of accountability for the other. However, a sense of guilt for past atrocities, the indignities we commit in our lifetimes, or the dereliction of our roles to advance equality only marginally impacts the entrenchment of White power and privilege today. Guilt produces defensiveness, powerlessness, and misdirected zeal. We become so layered with negative emotions that our hope for change wanes and our prospects of being the change fail to sprout. White guilt represents an earnest confrontation with race, racism, and, to some extent, racial truth-telling, but it abdicates the human contract to experiment with conversations and actions of repair. Guilt often leaves us feeling shock and horror, which produce only doubts, stress, pessimism, fear, and retreat.

When confronted by racial truths, we must probe our feelings to discern whether our guilt leads to reparative intercession or self-centered remorse. James W. Perkinson purports, "White self-confession requires more than mere self-naming or 'me too-ism.' It demands clear steps of conversion away from historical intentions and material privileges of White self-interest."[21] Inaction and apathy toward racism—unprocessed guilt—is White supremacy.

Even Black and Latinx individuals who "made it out" experience racial guilt—namely, survivors' remorse. By making it out,

I mean leaving neighborhoods disturbed by poverty, police over-presence, and disinvestment. Though upwardly mobile Black and Latinx folks never fully escape the reach of Whiteness and white noise, some do feel guilty for never looking and reaching back. Others feel the weight of buying into negative racial stereotypes.

White grief makes sense for processing and progressing beyond our crises of White sins. Seeing divinity in difference—racial difference as a gift—also means dying to one's previous relationship to Whiteness and going through the healing process to cultivate a new normal. Grief includes the negative feelings associated with death and loss—denial, anger, bargaining, and depression. It also creates a path toward healing, agency, and acceptance. Racism mulls, maims, and kills everything in its path, including White people. Instead of us dying to Whiteness, Whiteness must die to us. Without the death of Whiteness as an ideology, the truth of the divinity in difference—the promise of the *imago Dei*—never sees the light of day. Whiteness takes the air out of this transcendent truth, preventing us from embracing the colors of our flesh as gifts to one another and the whole.

America needs a death of Whiteness in order to save White, Black, and Brown flesh. In my tradition, Jesus beckons his followers to save their lives by losing their lives. In a world where Whiteness operates as a god, I read Jesus's call to death as an invitation to lose our Whiteness to save our humanity, which is sparked by the divine. This type of death leaves the body intact and creates a horizon for new life distinct from the deleterious resolve of Whiteness.

No one person will grieve the death of Whiteness the same as another. White grief, like grief after any loss of life, moves through a cycle of emotions, postures, resolutions, and actions. While I associate this form of racial healing with stages, White grief isn't always linear. Some people quickly transition from one stage to another, while others stall at one stage or another for prolonged periods of time. For various reasons, healing from our Whiteness may involve circumventing some steps altogether. Though frustrating, we may experience a given stage of White grief multiple times, causing us to assume we or the persons we support are not moving toward anti-racism and racial repair. We navigate the stages of grief to arrive at acceptance through several disciplines: lamentation, mapping, deference, confession, and contact.

A typical response to Whiteness and its necessary death is denial, what I call the first stage of White grief. Largely, this reflects the period when we refuse to come to terms with the scope of our racism or how we help perpetuate Whiteness. We retreat, hopefully only momentarily, from our previous "aha" moment of realizing our racial complicity. In an act of self-honesty, *lamentation* surfaces a series of authentic feelings. Fear, disappointment, and despair put us in touch with hardly explored facets of our humanity. To an extent, reparative intercession as lamentation forces us to attend to the ways Whiteness harms the host too. The ways we make space for shock and tears profoundly shape the process. Recognizing the sins of Whiteness leads us to pause, to deliberate what harms we have caused, ignored, and upheld. This emotional event essentially says something about how in touch we are with our *imago Dei*—the sacredness of our particularities. Indifference or, worse, delight in our sins of Whiteness creates a profound chasm between our life practices and our divine spark.

The second stage of White grief addresses anger. It is important to ask, "What took me so long to get here?" It is not rare to feel angry with ourselves or others as more of our personal history of discrimination and complicity come into focus. I recommend *mapping* the journey of racial awareness slowly, methodically, and faithfully. By tracing our lives back to our earliest racial memories, we start to mine our racial identity formation, a process we take up in chapter 4.

One of my earliest racial memories occurred in elementary school in La Marque, Texas. When I was a fifth grader at Simms Elementary, my class was mostly Black and Brown, which did not reflect the racial composition of the majority-white city. During lunch one afternoon, my classmates and I criticized the cafeteria food. For some reason, the conversation turned to the cafeteria service. We expressed appreciation for one of the staff members who always gave extra juice to my group of friends. During the conversation, I referred to the Latina worker as Mexican. One of my biracial friends responded, "No, she is from El Salvador, like my mother." "Isn't that all the same?" I retorted. I offended my friend that day, not because of a geographical fumble but because I erased the uniqueness of her Brownness. I was undoubtedly biased by what I had heard up to that point from adults, so I lumped many distinct Latinx peoples and cultures into one group.

When I consider my own White grief, I mentally map my way back to this moment. I ask, "Why did I believe this? From where did such ideas come? Who was harmed by my thinking and actions? Did my youth let me off the hook? What would have happened if no one had corrected me?"

The third stage of White grief is bargaining, a longing for the middle ground on race. It is a posture of racial neutrality like the placid category of nonracist. In the bargaining phase, we long to hold on to the power, privilege, and benefits of Whiteness as we reach for a new life. Without wresting free of these social advantages, we see racism as being external to us, leaving our racism intact. Though we voted for Barack Obama and Kamala Harris, marched down gentrified streets yelling "Black Lives Matter!" or married a Latinx person, we remain allied with racism if we benefit from practices designed to give an advantage to White people at the expense of non-White people. When we settle into a disposition of *deference*, we pursue a divestment from this delusional neutrality. Deference to the most vulnerable and unprotected unsettles any need to uphold false neutrality. By hearing the stories of impacted persons, we adjust to the idea that merely celebrating "Black culture" or volunteering to tutor Latinx children never fully accounts for the obligation to interrogate our beneficial relationship to Whiteness. The only way to counter our penchant to bargain our way to the middle—to a place of safety that allows us to pat ourselves on the back—is to humble ourselves at the feet of the most unprotected and violated. We either regress into Whiteness and white noise or progress into solidarity.

The fourth stage of White grief is depression, a profound sadness related to Whiteness remaining dead. We pass by the sepulchers of the status quo and ossuaries of oppressive Whiteness, resurrecting the racism we naively believed belonged to eras of old—slavery, the 1877–1923 nadir of race relations, or Jim and Jane Crow. As a condition for our humanity to live, Whiteness must not experience resurrection after we have resolved to terminate our relationship to its power and privilege. It is difficult to live without "something" we perceive to be so intimately woven into our sense of self. The bearers of White skin, eager to access a new life after Whiteness, feel the weight of this sadness as an existential crisis. White reparative intercessors carry a peculiar burden to live with White skin—the very marker of power and privilege in our nation—while saying a daily unequivocal "no" to the benefits. Pain emerges because they truly can and oftentimes want to reverse this death.

For White people specifically, healing in this stage means *confessing* what it means to be White. To be clear, Whiteness is an ideology, not an identity. Confessing Whiteness doesn't mean that one apologizes for one's ancestral bloodline and skin color. Whiteness operates as a system of ideas that produce, protect, and serve the interests of power and privilege that White people enjoy at the expense of non-White lives and opportunities. I identified Whiteness as sin—idolatrous, demonic, and segregationist—at work in us irrespective of our racial identities. Life is possible—we are possible—after the death of any ideology. In fact, the truly abundant life leads us past the graveside of Whiteness.

At the risk of oversimplifying, *confession*—one way of telling on ourselves—can take shape around a number of prompts arranged in no particular order. Immensely vital to the rhythm of cuing color, confession acknowledges racial differences as a social construct. We might state clearly, "My coworker is Honduran." "My child's teacher is Korean American." "That police officer is Black." "The judge was White." "The waiter is Black." "My congressman is White." "My best friends are White." "My primary care physician is Mexican American." After such a forthright observation, we can take a few moments to assess what their race means in the United States and what our race communicates in American public life. Then we can express how their race impacts our interactions with them. The more occasions we have for reflection, the more honest we find ourselves becoming. Confession also encompasses naming sins of Whiteness and associating them with real persons, places, and dates. This moves us out of our heads and into history. Real people carry the traumas or consequences of the sins of Whiteness irrespective of their racial identities.

These approaches to confession afford us the opportunity to interrogate how we conceptualize the *imago Dei*. We query, "What do my actions and speech reveal about how I understand human beings and the image of God?" Conceptions of the *imago Dei* link closely to our imaging of God. After a few years of practicing confession, I still find myself confronting internalized images of God as White. During these moments, I force myself to see and talk about God as something other than White (and male and imperialist and capitalist) without deracinating men who are powerful, White, and rich from the makeup of God's inspired creation. I identify God with the most unprotected among us as an act of confessing the hazards of the doctrine of Whiteness kept alive in and through me.

I previously addressed guilt in the journey toward racial awakening. Guilt is only one stage in a larger process toward antiracism and new life after the death of Whiteness. An immediate response to the guilt is increasing cross-racial *contact*. Isolation and internalization have abetted most of the failures in lives fixed in Whiteness. Grief furnishes an opportunity to heal from Whiteness with the support of other people. We are wired for communication and need to work this trauma out with others. However, this community should include persons we perceive as "other." Communities of reparative intercession aid us in racial healing, multiracial solidarity, and reconstructive action.

Finally, acceptance means we are fully alert to our racial realities even as we process the guilt, depression, anger, bargaining, and denial. Because grief is cyclical, the acceptance stage touches the previous feelings, dispositions, and challenges, but we experience them with a new resolve. Now these earlier stages validate our will to fight Whiteness within and orbiting around us. Acceptance says, "This work is exhausting, but my soul must have it." Acceptance confirms, "I made mistakes in my past life, but I'm more than my racism." Acceptance honors, "The Spirit of God is resident in all flesh, and I need to live that truth at all costs." Acceptance acknowledges, "Of course I want to fall apart over this. I lived a lie for so much of my life."

When we learn how Whiteness reduces us, we will jam the frequencies of its noise. Only by identifying how Whiteness works in us, around us, and on us can we go through the process of healing. The nudging of God's love for humanity insists we seal the catacombs of the decaying matter of White privilege. Only by making that last visit to the cemetery for the interment of Whiteness do we dare to reinvest in a life of multiracial sustainability.

Oneness without Sameness

We take the future of America for granted, as well as our own personal futures, because we fail to attend to the ways our addiction to exclusion and superiority cut us off from the living power of the Spirit resident in those barred from entry into our lives. Until people find a true north—a sense of self-direction unsullied by this history of White power—our society will not be aligned with the reign of God. The death of Whiteness gives us permission to resist the felt need to all be the same or to use Whiteness as the template for being human.

James Baldwin ponders, "I would like us to do something unprecedented: to create ourselves without finding it necessary to create an enemy."[22] People endowed with unearned, overexercised power need an enemy, a category of persons condemned by their god and controlled by their governments. The need for an enemy is sinful—demonic—because we're all born with equal value. We actually corrupt ourselves when we use the projected deficiencies of another to feed our sense of self. No one becomes good by making someone else bad. Are you really a whole person if your self-esteem begs for someone to hate or fear? What becomes of the civil in civilization if violence and inhumanity toward other humans are needed to protect it? To the moral demise of our nation and the impairment of our democracy, a politics of prejudice and a heritage of hate upend assumptive values of human equality and universal access to justice.

A fundamental property of God's creational design is that human beings bear the *imago Dei*—the image of God. Radically equal on an essential level, humans reflect the truth about God's diverse presence and personality. God created human oneness—not human sameness. Our differences fill out the story of God in the world. By grieving Whiteness and electing color-consciousness, we embrace the divinity of difference and find God in the face of the other.

Multiracial solidarity opens new horizons for ontological intimacy that allows humans to see, affirm, and advance racial difference in the work of racial repair. "Ontological intimacy," according to James Samuel Logan, "is the Christian confession that all things participate in the power of God's being through bonds of radical communion."[23] Ontological intimacy is not human sameness. Reparative intercession—namely, cues to color—upholds our rootedness in a single ground of being, God, and honors our difference as God-given. Spirituality and democracy clear space for the other to appear as they are. The future of civilization requires that people of faith participate in "the appearing acts" of those who are unseen in our midst—the dispossessed, disinherited, and disaffected. Using cues to color—seeing and embracing racial difference—is holy, divine, and sacred.

Emmanuel Levinas's understanding of face-to-face relationships helps to articulate the reparative rhythm of seeing color. According to the prominent French philosopher, we know God—the sacred—when we encounter the face of the other. Levinas purports, "The face is the other who asks me not to let him die alone, as if to do so were to become an accomplice in his death."[24] This notion signifies that people are responsible for one another face-to-face. When we understand the face of the other as the face of God, the face demands that we do more and be more for the ones who are not us. God invites us into a binding community of love through the face of the other. And we are prepared for reparative intercession when we see God, holiness, sacredness, and transcendence in the "not me." Life-enhancing beauty emanates from the faces of others. The degenerating moral health of America depends on our courage to see the other, stare exhaustively at the face of the other, and find transcendence in difference. We know and love God only to the extent that we consistently seek out personal encounters with the other.

No one leverages moral authority by reducing others to unfounded labels of immorality. We cease to journey toward full selfhood when we build ourselves up by breaking down others with labels like dangerous, uncivilized, and undeserving. The perception of the other as an enemy only proves the incompatibility of religious claims for human sameness and social practices of human hierarchy. We need to do the unprecedented thing: create ourselves without needing to create an enemy out of our siblings of different social identities—race, citizenship, class, gender, and sexuality.

"It's not my fault. Slavery was so long ago. Get over it."

Momentum to Encounter

Confronting the Histories of Whiteness

At our church's 2018 Martin Luther King Jr. Day commemoration, one of our White members who is a personal friend sat near the rear of the sanctuary. She was energized by eloquent speeches, the bring-down-the-house spirit of the choir, and the multiracial audience.

Noticing the discomfort of some of the politicians attending the event, she said to me, "They might as well have been holding a sign saying, 'I am not comfortable,' or 'I never saw this on *The Jeffersons*, or 'Alexa, get me out of here.' Sadly, this is the best we have, because many Republicans are now officially excused from even pretending to care." Per her norm, she lingered after the benediction to extend and receive hugs, but the MLK Day after-church experience was distinct from her weekly exchanges in our predominantly Black church.

"This night, I stayed in the sanctuary chatting with a politician who had approached me. Then the state legislator asked me, 'So you go to this church?'" After receiving confirmation that she worshiped at a Black church, the man—a White practicing Catholic—leaned toward her and whispered, "So, let me ask you something. The whole slavery thing. Like, I know it was horrible and everything, but do you ever just want to say, 'I mean, come on. It was hundreds of years ago. Can't we just get over it already?'"

Before my friend could gulp out a verbal response, the politician said, with a half-smile, "I know. I know. We're not supposed to say that."

She retorted, "No. We're not supposed to *think* it."

He rolled his eyes and said, "Yeah, I know."

The political leader was blind to the ways chattel slavery continuously affects American public life, economic prosperity, and social inequality. Because of where he lives, what he owns, and how he looks, he vies for a pass on white noise simply by showing up at a cultural event. Like so many could-be accomplices in racial repair, the political leader proved comatose to the legacy of slavery embedded in the lives of the people who elected him to serve.

White innocence runs through our national veins. White noise tells us we are innocent of and unaccountable for past horrific practices and death-making institutions that make up the bones of the nation we know.

Innocence That Blinds and Binds

The myth of innocence protects us from the truth of our tormenting present supported by the stilts of yesteryear. The less we know, the safer we appear, and the more "American" we act in public spaces as our othered siblings incur the empty promises of our nation's creeds. Averting our eyes from our charred racial history and present truth binds us as a nation doomed to lose spiritual vitality as we cling to stories of exceptionalism.

James Baldwin proffers:

> The people who settled the country had a fatal flaw. They could recognize a man when they saw one. They knew he wasn't . . . anything else but a man; but since they were Christian, and since they had already decided that they came here to establish a free country, the only way to justify the role this chattel was playing in one's life was to say that he was not a man. For if he wasn't a man, then no crime had been committed. That lie is the basis of our present trouble . . . a man being oppressed by other men who did not even have the courage to admit what they were doing.[1]

In this sense, innocence amounts to sin. When we avoid the truth of our past and our present, we give credence to a racial hierarchy crushing those at the bottom. The only path toward moral maturity includes unswaddling the garments of innocence that keep us warm as white noise aids our sociopolitical sleep.

White privilege hinges on White ignorance as innocence and non-White silence as innocence. Charles Mills writes, "The Racial Contract prescribes for its signatories an inverted epistemology (a way of knowing), an epistemology of ignorance, a particular pattern of localized and global cognitive dysfunctions (which are psychologically and socially functional), producing the ironic outcome that whites will in general be unable to understand the world they themselves have made."[2] This brand of ignorance as innocence allows us to rinse our hands of the quandary of marginalized people and divert our attention from the brutality of yesterday and the racial pain of today.

The unearned benefits White people enjoy and the unearned disadvantages non-White people endure are the result of centuries of injustice. Genocidal forced labor built American economic greatness while preventing American moral goodness. Nonetheless, the innocence myth offers a faux protection from the truth of Black disinheritance and from the new forms that structural racism takes in each historical chapter. Our national innocence is a lie. It is a lie that imminently threatens the futures of all our lives. From within our tenuous comfort zones, we fail to realize that our very humanity slowly but surely crumbles to pieces when we see pain and say nothing.

A Historical Witness of Christian Whiteness

American Christianity has helped to shield us from our racial truth, has fed our illusions of innocence, and has baptized our bigotry with Bible verses. White noise reverberates off the walls of many houses of worship. Myriad US churches, across racial and class lines, center values on personal piety, individual responsibility, and otherworldly salvation, obscuring systemic inequality and oppression. From Texas to New York, I have worked with Christians in predominantly Black and Brown congregations who need a new language and new frameworks to combat racism and the religious right's monopolizing of Christianity.

Before the Confederacy's secession from the Union in 1860, the Methodist Episcopal Church formally split over the issue of slavery in 1844. White Baptists split over the same moral crisis a year later. These splits allowed the denominations' Southern factions (the Southern Methodist Episcopal Church and the Southern Baptist Church) to maintain their support of the peculiar institution of slavery. In 1829 David Walker wrote in his *Appeal*, "Have not the Americans read the Bible in their hands? Do they believe it? Surely they do not. See how they treat us in open violation of the Bible!"[3] Slaveholding and Jim Crow Christianity closely resemble contemporary White Christian racism and colorblindness, which support prison and military industrial complexes, anti-immigration sentiment, and police brutality. History notwithstanding, in a 2019 survey, six in ten US adults (62 percent) somewhat or strongly disagreed with the notion that churches are complicit in racial subjugation.[4]

So much of American evangelicalism is White thought protecting White political power. Valid Lazar Puhalo says, "Religion as ideology is one of the most evil and destructive forces on earth. If ever Satan created a weapon of mass destruction, his greatest success was in leading people to degrade faith into religion and religion into ideology. Binding religion to politics is to secularise the Church. It is a re-crucifixion of Christ and an utter betrayal of His Gospel."[5] Churches and Christian leaders, through silence or full-throated endorsements, have allied with racist institutions, structures, and political leaders in every period of European presence in the Americas. Racism courses through the bloodstream of US Christianities through congregational leadership, moral facades of political interests, sermonic rhetoric, and numbing silence.

From Cotton Mather and D. L. Moody to Billy Sunday and Jerry Falwell, White Christian racism has amplified anti-Black policies—a history of inaction still alive in the backdrop of a new generation of personalities like Franklin Graham and Paula White. In the 2020 election, more than three-fourths (76 percent) of White evangelicals and "born-again" Christians still cast a ballot for former president Trump,[6] down only five percentage points from the 81 percent of electoral support they delivered him in 2016.[7] While serving as the leader of the free world, former president Trump created a litany of despicable, morally incorrigible white noise: "Mexicans are rapists and drug dealers. And some, I assume, are good people."[8] "All Haitians have AIDS."[9] "Nigerians will never go back to their huts."[10] African nations are "sh–hole countries."[11] While some White evangelical leaders distanced themselves from Trump's comments, countless pastors retreated to silence or sacralized his reactions. Some even alluded to the former president as a savior-type.

White evangelicalism poses obstacles to racial justice and repair because of its inability to comprehend the systemic nature of Whiteness. *Divided by Faith*, authored by Michael O. Emerson and Christian Smith, explores the racialized assumptions of White evangelicalism in the United States.[12] Emerson and Smith present White evangelicals, nearly 90 percent of self-identified evangelicals in America, as White conservative Protestants who believe in (1) the ultimate authority of Scripture, (2) the salvific death of Christ, (3) Christ as the exclusive path to eternal life, and (4) the importance of evangelizing.[13] The authors purport that White evangelicals practice "engaged orthodoxy," which compels them to go public with their beliefs. Overall, they champion strict heteropatriarchal family values and conservative public policies.

Emerson and Smith navigate the theological and mental prisms through which evangelicals tend to approach the "race problem." The three prisms the authors name include the following: (1) *accountable freewill individualism*, which accents a politics of responsibility and self-direction; (2) *relationalism*, which places a premium on interpersonal relationships and a personal relationship with Jesus; and (3) *anti-structuralism*, which is closely linked to freewill individualism and vehemently rejects understanding and accepting structures as influencers on lived experience.[14] These foundational assumptions stymie reparative intercession.[15] White evangelicals almost exclusively conceptualize racism as individual, isolated practices instead of structural, discursive, and institutional realities.

Colorblind Christianity reads Black socioeconomic inequality as the result of individual decisions, poor human associations, and individual racists. White evangelicals overwhelmingly explain the Black-White socioeconomic gap as a by-product of Black culture and limited motivation. They perceive Black people, including fellow Christians, as violators of critical tenets of White conservative Christianity: personal responsibility and healthy relationality.[16] According to the authors' findings, White evangelicals also categorize Black people as sinners. They sin "both by relying on programs rather than themselves and by shifting blame to structurally based reasons of inequality."[17] This colorblind Christianity blames the impacted communities for the racial wealth gap, education lags, hyper-incarceration, and unemployment.

In July 2020, during the racial justice uprisings following the deaths of George Floyd and Breonna Taylor, roughly two in five US Christians definitively asserted that the nation has a race problem.[18] A fifth saw no problem with race in the United States, and 57 percent of White Christians (and a fifth of Black Christians) disagreed with the statement, "Historically, the US has been oppressive to minorities."[19] In a 2019 study marking the four hundredth year of Black sojourn in America, the Barna Group found that three in five White Christians saw the nation's race problem as an individual matter, limiting racism to personal beliefs and behaviors. As cities teemed with anti-racist vigor, only a quarter of White Christians said they were motivated to address racism. A quarter of White Christians expressed a personal responsibility to care for people who face discrimination through financial or other resources (24 percent) and in-person service (25 percent), while only 14 percent said churches should be engaged in either approach.[20]

Tell the Truth and Shame the Devil

As a college freshman, I attended the World Council of Churches (WCC) with a delegation of other student ministers from Morehouse College. The delegation was organized by Dr. Lawrence Edward Carter Sr., founding dean of the Martin Luther King Jr. International Chapel. Impressed by the storied history of the WCC, I walked the exhibition hall enamored by the international presence, the senior leadership from every major Christian communion, and the gravitas of the attendees. Dean Carter ushered us from room to room, unpacking the significance of what we were experiencing, underscoring what a rarity it was for clergy our age to be present for such consequential conversations and decision-making.

Following one afternoon session, Dean Carter pulled the twelve of us into a corner of the lobby to reminisce about the late

Rev. Gardner C. Taylor—the dean of Black preachers and legendary pastor of the Concord Baptist Church of Christ in Brooklyn, New York. As Carter spoke passionately about Taylor's poetic imagination and command of the English language, a White Lutheran pastor interrupted the exchange. "What brings you to the annual session?" After learning that we attended Morehouse, she nodded to the legacy of the college as a pipeline for socially conscious Black clergy. Swelling with pride, we listened to her talk about a few Morehouse men with whom she had worked. Then she said, "What were you guys talking about? Did I interrupt something important?"

Slightly annoyed by the disruption, I replied, "We were talking about Dr. Gardner Calvin Taylor, a luminary of the Black church."

She responded by telling us about when she heard him speak at a session of the WCC. "You mentioned the Black church," she added. "As we continue to achieve racial reconciliation, will the Black church ever cease to exist? I long for the day when we don't need the Black church."

While we all paused, puzzled, one of the upperclassmen countered, "Will the White church cease to exist?"

She did not seem to recognize that she belonged to a White church, with a history of White supremacy and White Christian terror that mandated the need for Black congregations.

As self-assuming protagonists, White Christians willfully ignore our national racial history and the contributions churches have made to the pains we know today. Though many White Christians feign ignorance, White Christianities have history, forms, and structures that shape the present.

When white noise entices us to look away from the repulsion of racism, we must practice the momentum to encounter. This rhythm dares us to confront the histories that we live within and that live within us. A rigorous confrontation of the past alive in the present rejects the white noise that allows us to feel that "It's not my fault. Slavery was so long ago. Get over it."

A third of White Christians (33 percent) resign themselves to the belief that "there's nothing the Church should do" to respond to anti-Black racism. [21] As we recover from the post-truth era of Trumpism, truth-telling (racial parrhesia) and reparative intercession are revolutionary. The soul of America is predicated on our willingness to tell the truth and to tell it during off news cycles. The salvation of our society calls for truth-telling from politicians and preachers, educators and students, and parents and employers. A poignant colloquialism birthed out of the Black religious experience seems most appropriate: "Tell the truth and shame the devil." Naming our sins is a crucial step to transcending them.

White noise like "The past is the past" is a chronological argument removing the person from issues of racism today. White noise like "I/my family didn't own slaves" is a culpability argument inferring that only extreme forms of racial violence meet the litmus test for racism. Both forms of historical avoidance are an attempt by the speaker to distance themselves from the truth of their current day while feeding on the rotten fruit of previous days. However, history is never the past. As Maya Angelou said, "History, despite its wrenching pain, cannot be unlived, but if faced with courage, need not be lived again." [22] Reparative intercession draws from a history of the present, which maps out how history lives in current social practices, structural inequalities, and individual perceptions.

Racism is specific to a given historical moment and creates nuanced strictures and structures distinct from previous eras. Adolph Reed reminds us, "The reflexive attribution of today's battery of racial inequalities to a generic, transhistorical racism or white supremacy actually serves to shift attention away from the discrete, historically specific mechanisms that inform actual racialized social outcomes." [23] The current historical moment of Whiteness—in post-Obama neoliberal America—showcases unemployment and wage disparities, healthcare unaffordability and food apartheid, digital divides and voter suppression, mass incarceration and televised police killings, education inequality and COVID-19–related disruptions, the Tea Party and MAGA, and liberal paternalism and the Religious Right. However, these current social issues have histories; they emerged from decades of policy strategies and practices of previous eras.

The lives we lead owe a peculiar debt to the social and the structural forces some of us enjoy the mental luxury of pretending do not exist. A history of systemic and individual, overt and covert racial injustice makes racial disparities appear natural and inevitable. The past in the present is killing us.

Reparative intercession questions what we take for granted by mining the continuity between the past and the present. Here I am imploring us to ask, as a spiritual practice, why the present is as it is and what aspects of the past linger and help us explain our racial conditions. A history of the present helps us talk about how the contemporary situation emerged and how we might forge a world less mired by the abuses of racial injustice. The momentum to encounter—the transformative confrontation of history—invites both individuals and institutions to truthful explorations, immersive exchanges, emotional attentiveness, sacred sensitivity, and legacy locating.

Practices for Momentous Encounter

Truthful Explorations

The momentum to encounter necessitates unpacking our national racial story through *truthful explorations*. Research confirms that educating White people, particularly children, about the nation's racial history—namely, four centuries of anti-Black exclusion and violence—lessens racial bias. An honest historical excavation of America runs headlong through African enslavement and indigenous slaughter, which served as down payment for carving out a new world for Whiteness to experiment with predation and exploitation as means of power-building. It is difficult to stomach when our media and schools, government and churches peddle a steady stream of stories that make Americans the heroes. Anger, resentment, disbelief, and fear are logical responses to the truth living beneath the surface of our founding documents, political luminaries, military prowess, elections, and pioneering government structures.

Truthfully exploring our history requires admitting the ways White supremacy baked itself into the laws of the land. Since the colonial period, lawmakers, judges, and the "expert class" have constructed Whiteness in our nation through key moments that continue to weigh on our lives today. Some landmark moments in American history come to mind for a practice of truthful exploration.

Ugly History: Color-Coded Citizenship

The ugly history of US citizenship reveals a color-coded schema and hegemonic conspiracy that are anything but colorblind law. Not only does the law know color, it also makes meaning of race and its relationship to power and protection. This political construction of Whiteness and rights on these shores started with British colonists and reached the heights of the US Supreme Court in the mid-nineteenth century.

In the early days of the European colonial experiment, Virginia lawmakers wrote Whiteness into Christianity and White Christianity into law. In 1670, Virginia law forbade Native Americans and free Africans in America from purchasing Christians, while legalizing their right to purchase other non-Europeans irrespective of religion. The policy read in part, "*It is enacted* that noe negro or Indian though baptised and enjoyned their owne freedome shall be capable of any such purchase of Christians, but yet not debarred from buying any of their owne nation."[24] The pre-Constitution Virginia statute gave Whiteness political and theological protection and power, which crudely survived the formation of a new republic and the Bill of Rights to the US Constitution. The 1670 law ratified the assumption that White people owned Christianity, despite the fact that the Christian faith was born out of the imagination, genius, and state-sponsored death of a non-European Jesus. The law made a distinction between the enslaveable and the Christian—namely, between Black and Native people and White people. The House of Burgesses cast Blacks and Natives, even if they were baptized followers of Jesus, as members of nations incongruent with the nations of Christians. Earlier laws passed in Virginia allowed Christian Whiteness to protect poor White people from the dispossession, captivity, and brutality reserved for slaves—a peculiar category of servitude in the "New World" by the mid-seventeenth century.

Leading an independent nascent nation, the framers of the Constitution also wrote Whiteness into Americanness. Article 1, section 2 of the US Constitution, ratified in 1788, stipulated that enslaved persons—with no need to mention their race—be counted as three-fifths of a free person as a way to apportion taxes and congressional representation. While the non-slaveholding states argued against the slave population being counted at all, the three-fifths compromise swelled southern federal power. Both sides of the debate—the slaveholding and the non-slaveholding—reduced the slave to real estate, property to be managed and moved for the economic benefit of White elites and the young nation. Both sides of the debate damned the political agency and freedom of Black lives.

Two years after the Constitution was ratified, the first Congress, in its second session, took up its first debate on the meaning of US citizenship. The Naturalization Act of 1790 limited applications for citizenship to "free white persons, being of good character, and living in the United States for two years." As a matter of self-interest and power-guarding, the all-White male legislature restricted citizenship to people of their same social location—White male property owners. The new nation's political structure endowed a sense of entitlement and belonging to a narrow version of Whiteness—propertied, patriarchal Whiteness.

The 1857 decision of *Dred Scott v. Sandford* epitomizes the truth living under American exceptionalism and a color-coded legal system. This legal battle for freedom, started in 1846, raised the question "Whose rights (and bodies) are protected under the law?"

John Emerson purchased Scott, born as a slave in Virginia, from Peter Blow. Emerson took Scott to Illinois and the Wisconsin Territory, where slavery was illegal. When Scott was taken to Missouri, which promoted a "once free, always free" precedent, Scott sued for his freedom on the grounds that he had lived in "free" territories and, therefore, had been freed and was legally no longer a slave.

After losing in the lower federal court and the Missouri Supreme Court, Scott sued the United States in an attempt to gain his freedom. In the ruling, decided 7 to 2 against Scott, Chief Justice Roger Taney wrote that members of the African race were "of an inferior order and altogether unfit to associate with the white race, either in social or political relations, and so far inferior that they had no rights which the white man was bound to respect."[25] A heinous denial of Black citizenship, a few long years prior to the outbreak of the Southern rebellion against the United States, the Scott case underscored what Black people knew since disembarking the hulls of ships bearing religious names and exiting the auction blocks: US citizenship was a White privilege. The high court's ruling unequivocally denied citizenship to enslaved persons, their progeny, and freed Black persons. This is ugly history ripe to help us make sense of the mess in which we currently live.

Ugly History: No Honorary Whiteness

Leaving the Punjab region of India, Bhagat Singh Thind immigrated to the United States in 1913 to matriculate at the University of California, Berkeley. When the United States entered World War I, Thind enlisted in the army. His superiors acknowledged him for his exceptional service. While in active duty, he applied for US citizenship in Oregon, which a district court granted in 1920. However, soon after he received naturalization status, a naturalization examiner contested his eligibility for citizenship on the grounds that he was not a free White person or a free person of African descent. These were the requirements for citizenship stipulated by the Naturalization Acts of 1790 and 1870 respectively.

During the 1923 Supreme Court case, Thind argued that, as a native of north India (Caucasia), he must be permitted to identify racially as Caucasian. During Thind's lifetime, *Caucasian* identity included the high caste of people from India. He employed his Hindu caste status to argue relationality to Whiteness. The SCOTUS opinion ruled that being Caucasian proved to be insufficient grounds for US citizenship, since "the average man knows perfectly well that there are unmistakable and profound differences."[26] The high court rhetorically drew attention to the phenotypic dissimilarities between White people and persons from India, while also likely evoking the specter of linguistic, religious, and cultural distinctions. The government confiscated Thind's properties and victimized other Indian immigrants under laws prohibiting non-Whites from owning property. The 9 to 0 ruling against Thind further dramatized the US government's power to construct the meaning of Whiteness to the devastation of non-White freedoms and protections.

There is no honorary Whiteness, contrary to our professional approximations, collegiate pedigrees, or cultural performances. Ugly history disabuses us of our wanton desire to cling for dear life to American innocence and colorblind pretentions.

From 1670, Whiteness came to be squarely synonymous with Americanness. Despite the impressive string of amendments designed to widen freedoms, the bones of our republic's Constitution reify non-White disinheritance and unprotection. That is our ugly history awaiting our truthful exploration. Today's mass disparities and the significance of racial difference are rooted in this history of color-coded jurisprudence irrespective of our fictional tales of colorblindness.

The legacy of this politically constructed definition of Whiteness inhibits our nation from seeing Black bodies beyond the benefits of their labor and searingly pejorative stereotypes. Truth-telling and truth-consuming disavow our avoidance, redactions, and the myths meant to preserve our innocence—moral and emotional distance from the legacy of terror.

Immersive Exchanges

Confronting history like this merits *immersive exchanges*. By this, I mean sharing and workshopping what we've learned. Conversations about specific historical events, as a principle of reparative intercession and racial parrhesia (truth-telling), create pressure to reach across the lines that divide us. Every fearless act of reparative intercession closes an escape hatch positioned to let us off the hook for the racism that fires from every corner of our lives.

Communities of reparative intercession help us imagine a future of racial healing, multiracial solidarity, and reconstructive action. As I previously mentioned regarding White grief, the support of others helps the healing process. We are wired for communication and need to work toward a future of awareness in community. Our irrational obsession with innocence cancels the prospect of encountering God in the other, but acceptance of the death of Whiteness allows us to see God in the face of the other. Wrestling with history becomes a sacred rite when it opens new doors to relationships otherwise unpursued.

In *The Search for Common Ground*, Howard Thurman muses, "Meaningful and creative shared experiences between people can be more compelling than all of the faiths, fears, concepts and ideologies that separate them. And, if these experiences can be multiplied and sustained over a sufficient duration of time, then any barrier that separates one person from another can be undermined and eliminated."[27] Building community undermines the power of White sin, the social force that segregates, impairs human oneness, reinforces the innocence myth, and distributes power unevenly. We confront ugly history together as an ethic of persistent neighborliness (a concept we return to in chapter 3). Immersive exchanges move us toward community anchored in interdependence and mutual becoming. This mode of engagement reduces social distance and power differences.

Emotional Attentiveness

Reparative intercession is a vocation of disruption and discomfort that allows the momentum to encounter to be an opportunity to name our feelings out loud. We need to create spaces where we can disagree, share a diversity of perspectives, and even miscommunicate in search of common ground. After a critically honest excavation of our ugly national history, it is important to voice questions related to our discoveries: "What brings me pride?" "What causes me pain?" "To what am I indifferent?"

By virtue of such an embittered history, we all occupy a fragile place in the American reality. The narrative arc of the American experiment hinges on the entry and contributions of immigrants and "imports"—Black bodies trafficked as chattel. In the sticky humidity of a Southern night, human traders herded enslaved Africans through the woods from the riverside docks to the market square. I am a descendant of imports from the Tikar people of Cameroon, the Bubi people of Bioko Islands, and the Nuna people of Burkina Faso. I am a descendent of people who were living imports. For the first thirty years of my life, I did not know this history. I knew abstractly that White people stuffed my people in the bottom of ships on the western shores of Africa, but like so many Black Americans, I lacked any sense of my personal background. In 2017, however, I learned my true African ancestry and now share it in every training.

I am proud to finally know how I connect to Africa, to know a lineage beyond the ugly history of whips and chains, auction blocks and nooses. The first time I shared this ancestral finding publicly, I decided not to choke down the tears or deny the lump in my throat. I unleashed emotions that were long sealed up along-side my stolen identity in front of a group of mostly White male ministers in Atlanta. These tears testified to the death of ignorance for me and the death of pretentious innocence in Whiteness. These were tears of pride-soaring awareness. I made history personal that day. And an eerie quietness commanded the room. I closed that segment in silence as the workshop participants, tongues muted, darted off.

Later, over lunch catered by Paschal's Restaurant—an iconic Black culinary establishment in the historic West End—the silence finally broke. One participant sat down next to me avoiding eye contact. I put my head down, looked at my phone, and started surfing Twitter in an attempt to ward off the awkwardness. I took a sip of sweet tea and inhaled a piece of cornbread. "This tastes like my memi's cornbread," I blurted out. The White man seated next to me said, "I loved my mom's cornbread. She learned her recipe from one of our neighbors, a Black neighbor." I nodded with approval and said, "I get it."

The gentleman then acknowledged his appreciation of how knowing my history engendered so much passion and pride. He continued by disclosing, for the first time in his life, that his an-cestors owned slaves and operated a farm after emancipation. For him, shame accompanied his family history. Counter to my experience and response in learning about my ancestral footprint, his pride died the day he discovered his ancestors owned slaves and that the wealth he inherited likely stemmed from said organized dehumanization. I responded, "That's the point of telling history. The death of innocence and ignorance." After another twenty minutes of exchange, the descendent of slaveholding White people expressed how talking openly about his familial past brought him a sense of peace regarding his family that he hadn't experienced in years. It's amazing what cornbread unlocked for us. I shared my pride, and he shared his shame. Cornbread welcomed us into a space of *emotional attentiveness*.

Sacred Sensitivity

Sacred sensitivity beckons us to listen to and honor the feelings of the other. Racial history is hard to digest for all Americans but exponentially harder for those on the receiving side of its terror, displacement, and exclusion. In this framing, reparative intercession entails listening in a way that is sensitive to and disrupts oppression. This means seeing persons who are othered as bearers of truth.

Spurred by my interest in reclaiming a revolutionary practice of the Jesus movement, I created the Public Love Organizing and Training (PLOT) project, a fifteen-hour anti-racism educational program aimed at mobilizing a network of Black, White, and Latinx Christians in anti-incarceration advocacy. The program explores (1) racism as a form of structural power that advantages some and oppresses others along the lines of skin color and racial identity, (2) race as a social construct with grave implications for religious, political-economic, and social lives, (3) mass incarceration as a form of social control in the lineage of chattel slavery and Jim Crow segregation, and (4) the ways in which US Christianities are complicit in maintaining racial caste and mass incarceration as racialized forms of social control.

In each PLOT experience, the participants dedicate attention to US history via a timeline of events and narratives placarded around the room. The more than fifty moments of racial history include the arrival of Black persons in 1619; the 1790 Naturalization Act; the Nat Turner Rebellion; the Southern Homestead Act; the Tulsa Massacre; the civil rights movement; and the respective elections of Obama and Trump. The attendees walk around the room of history for twenty-five minutes. As they grapple with the unsettling details of violence, hate, and disinheritance in silence, they write down their thoughts on Post-it notes and leave them on the wall beneath the pieces of history.

Seated in a circular arrangement, the participants then prepare to share with the group by ruminating on the following questions:

- What did I learn?
- How did I feel?
- What was difficult to see?
- What happened during my lifetime?
- Can I trace a lasting impact?
- Who were the victims? Who were the victors?
- What role did Christianity play in the horror and correction?
- Where was God?

During a group session in Dallas, Ronald—a thirty-three-year-old youth pastor—lingered at the history wall for longer than the exercise allowed. He paced from sign to sign, rereading the historical narratives again and again. He stalled at the picture and write-up of Emmett Till. A mob of White Mississippians lynched the fourteen-year-old Black boy in 1955 for allegedly making a pass at a White woman.

After about ten minutes, I prompted Ronald to rejoin the cohort for the group reflection phase. As he walked toward the circle, he stopped in his tracks and revisited one final image posted on the wall—a picture of Trayvon Martin. I invited him once more to return to the group, under the conviction that his peers might prove to be the best containers for whatever seemed to be bubbling beneath his silence. Once he was back in the group, one of the attendees made notice of a tear welling in the corner of his eye. He waved off the attention assertively with both arms and expressed an unwillingness to share. Cameron, one of the three White women in the circle, spoke up, "Ron, I cannot fathom what you are chewing on, but I think this is a good time for sacred silence." Perhaps she needed the silence to decompress too, or perhaps she sensed that a conversation at that moment might be too much for Ron. The group held space for what felt like an hour but was more like five minutes.

Then Ronald interrupted the silence of the group. "Why are they still doing this to us?" He linked the terrorism responsible for Till's death and that responsible for the shooting of Trayvon. He asked, "When will we be human enough, lovable enough, smart enough to no longer experience this type of evil?" The group nodded in affirmation of the pain living within his questions. The group centered his feelings, and the silence unlocked his tongue, allowing him to rail against the nation's history of White vigilantism. Sacred sensitivity in the form of silence and patience served as the precondition to hear from a Black man wrestling with the ongoing threat of death. The group functioned as a brave space, allowing him to show up and speak transparently, after exploring ugly history.

Legacy Locating

Legacy locating involves making deliberate connections between the past and the present. We must trace the trajectory of the lasting impact of past events, policies, phenomena, and experiences. After we unearth the record of what has happened, deliberate with the other, sit with what is hard to accept, and hold feelings as sacred, the next step is to crown the truth that the present has a history. The innumerable social crises of our day begin to make sense and appear inevitable due to this history. We deploy the interior resources requisite to make sense of these crises by legacy locating. The present comes out of the past in myriad ways. When we engage in legacy locating, we (1) identify a problem of interest, (2) describe the features of said problem, (3) ponder whether there is a historical antecedent to the current problem, and (4) draw lines of connection between then and now.

I stumbled into legacy locating as a sophomore in college. The morning after my mom informed me that a judge had sentenced my favorite older cousin to five years in prison, I woke up at 4 a.m. in a panic. I grabbed my cell phone from the nightstand and texted my cousin in extreme disbelief that this young man from a God-fearing household was headed "up the river" to a notorious

Texas prison. I stared at my phone for a response that never came. Fully submerged facedown under my bed linens, I forcefully threw the phone onto the hardwood floor of the room.

Moments later, I emerged from the bed intent on figuring out why this had happened. Careful not to disturb the sleep of my housemates, I tiptoed down the stairs in search of my backpack. I walked into our living room, nearly tripping over someone's Air Jordans. Spotting a notepad on the makeshift coffee table, I picked it up with no ideas of what to do next. After sinking into the couch, I impulsively wrote down everything I remembered about my cousin's friends and neighborhood. Then I wrote down everything that came to mind about cops, courts, and prisons. I knew the culture of over-policing in certain communities and school campuses. I remembered listening to people complain about the docket load of public defenders in Georgia. I assumed the same was true for Texas courts. I permitted these memories and details to fall from my pen. Eventually, I commenced writing down questions and notes related to what I did not know at the time. Later that day, I took my unanswered questions with me to the library. I started reading and filling out the history in that notepad. This was the start of what I now call legacy locating. Unexplained grief taught me the makings of legacy locating fifteen years ago.

Let us briefly consider the emergencies related to our nation's wealth gap and carceral culture, both of which are married to structural racism. The egregious racial wealth gap today is explained by legacy locating through slavery and Jim Crow wage theft. Similarly, Black mass incarceration today is explained by legacy locating through vagrancy laws, convict leasing, and law-and-order politics.

The White Sin of a Racial Wealth Gap

Why are wealth and poverty so palpably and demonstrably racialized in our cities? The unprecedented wealth of the United States and its racialized disparities undeniably find root in the forced labor of Africans. The abysmal racial wealth gap between

Black and White Americans is a product of history, not merely current income and education trends. Though Black people compose roughly 13 percent of the US population, they possess only four percent of the nation's wealth.[28] The median wealth (the difference between a household's assets and debts) of a White family is around $189,100, while the average Black family wallows with a mere $24,100.[29] For every $100 in White family wealth, Black families have just $12.78. Eight generations after the legal end to the chattel system, the 4 percent of the nation's wealth owned by Black people represents a shameful increase from the 0.5 percent that Black people owned in 1863, when the majority of Blacks were still property themselves.[30] This remains true even with the passage of the Thirteenth, Fourteenth, and Fifteenth Amendments, a couple of civil rights acts, the Voting Rights Act of 1965, and the Fair Housing Act of 1968.

If some disruptive cosmic force broke into time and froze the average wealth of a White household today, Black households would have to work, earn, save, and invest for 228 years before they found economic parity with their White counterparts. This is the evolving, yet-to-be interrupted legacy of 246 years of chattel slavery. Slavery's capitalism merely gave way to the racial capitalism of predatory sharecropping, convict leasing, and redlining. During Jim Crow apartheid, a manifestation of White sin, employers undercompensated Black workers due to race and undervalued skill sets, which was connected to poorly funded public schools and barriers to certain vocational education opportunities. The redlining conspiracy between racist banks and the real estate world underwrote Black dispossession by denying them homeownership. Housing equity makes up two-thirds of average household wealth. Therefore, Black middle-class households with earning power equal to or greater than White middle-class households are more vulnerable to economic hardship because of the privation of generational inheritances that their White counterparts count on. The wealth gap instantiates the hierarchy of lives and bodies, placing White people, especially White men, on top as the model of humanity to which all should aspire.

The White Sin of Mass Incarceration

Though I did not command the depth necessary to understand it when I was twenty and trying to figure out why my cousin was doing a bid, Black incarceration knows the soil of chattel slavery too. Michelle Alexander, in her seminal work *The New Jim Crow: Mass Incarceration in the Age of Colorblindness*, states, "More African American adults are under correctional control today—in prison or jail, on probation or parole—than were enslaved in 1850, a decade before the Civil War began."[31] This is due to a politically manufactured "drug crisis." Though the United States is only 5 percent of the world's population, it houses 25 percent of the world's incarcerated people. From 1865 to 1968, a total of 184,901 Americans entered state and federal prisons. From 1968 to the early 1980s, America housed 251,107 in its prisons.[32] Today, incarceration sits at 2.2 million people, half of whom are Black and Brown, even though Black people make up only 13 percent of the population and Latinx people 18 percent. Startlingly, incarceration has increased by 943 percent in the last fifty years. According to Alexander and some social scientists, the racialized war on drugs, which was augmented during the Reagan administration, quadrupled the percentage of prison sentences related to the possession and vending of narcotics.[33]

From slavery into emancipation, the White imagination converted Black lives from chattel to criminal. Both identifications relate that free Black bodies pose dangers to Whiteness, as those bodies purportedly contradict a perverted formulation of natural law memorialized in our very social order. The white noise of Black dehumanization, a symptom of the sin of Whiteness, spawned from the shadows of antebellum plantations and solidified in the wake of the Reconstruction era. Scholarly research, popular speeches, and media—then and now, to a comparable degree—seared the image of the Black criminal and the conflation of Blackness and danger into the national psyche after abolition and Reconstruction. From the 1880s to the present, the criminalization of Black bodies has ratified this de facto segregation and neo-slavery through US prisons and post-incarceration repression. Post-Reconstruction policies essentially rendered Black life illegal, dragging Black bodies out of free space consecrated for White people through Black codes, vagrancy schemes, and convict leasing.[34]

The veneer of doctored scientific evidence concerning Black inferiority could no longer justify the national project of disinheriting Black life. Therefore, drawing on newly created academic journals, popular periodicals, and growing lecture circuits, popular forms of nineteenth-century media shifted the narrative concerning Black inferiority from scientific to moral arguments, thus underscoring a bond of racial solidarity between new European immigrants and American-born White people chiefly determined by a shared fear of Black men as criminals.[35]

For White Americans of every ideological stripe—from radical southern racists to northern progressives—"African American criminality became one of the most widely accepted bases for justifying prejudicial thinking, discriminatory treatment, and/or acceptance of racial violence as an instrument of public safety,"[36] according to Khalil Gibran Muhammad. The aforementioned US culture of criminalization shelters Whiteness, which courses through the veins of mass incarceration, and the "divine right" to re-create a White Christian republic by normalizing the disappearance and removal of Black bodies in the name of criminal justice.

A vestige of antebellum American logic, the Black person lives as the synecdoche of American disinheritance. In the logic of Whiteness, which undergirds all American institutions, Black people were created to be ruled. According to Kelly Brown Douglas, "The black body as chattel is the core element in the construction of the inherently guilty black body."[37] The Black body as chattel signifies that Black people lack the right to own their bodies and labor. The construct of Black criminality safeguards the social logic of treating Black bodies as valued commodities of Whiteness in an era disgusted by slavery but needing to hold on to racial caste. Black criminalization—a viral contagion of White supremacy—functions as the excuse needed to protect systemic racism as an acceptable approach to racial control and social domination, recruiting the nation's courts, law enforcement agencies, financial entities, educational institutions, and religious communions to do the bidding of Whiteness.

For instance, the criminalization of Black bodies explains Black dispossession like mass incarceration. Criminal justice in America, guided by racialized punitive logic, legitimates de facto segregation, labor market discrimination, the stigma of criminality,[38] residential injustice, and educational funding. This form of racial stigmatization creates a paradox: White prejudice exists because of Black criminality; Black criminality exists because of White racism. The criminalization of Blackness as a given social pathology, though fundamentally racist, works to scapegoat White apathy and terror in the name of American innocence. The stigma of criminality offers a defense of aggressive policing, shoot-first protocols, and mandatory minimums.

Once during a panel discussion about mass incarceration at a small liberal arts college, a White minister responded to me, "All I hear is the problem but not the solution." While so often academics experience the paralysis of analysis on certain pressing issues, her prompt toward solution-directed conversation betrayed her real intentions. She desperately desired to avoid the discomfort of confronting the history of the present. Unquestionably, the problems of racism deserve robust conversations, strategic planning sessions, and direct action toward solutions. However, talking honestly with and listening to impacted persons and studying the nature and manifestations of Whiteness can be seeds that grow into solutions. If race talk is more than so many White people can bear, then they may want to dare to imagine how much harder it is for people victimized by racism to live with it.

"I've had it hard too, but I worked hard."

3

Pattern Recognition

Honoring Our Interdependence

A close friend, a pastor of a predominantly Black church in the Midwest, was invited to a gathering of pastors in 2020 to build a coalition of politically engaged clergy. A notable Black pastor organized the event in a famed majority-Black city to dramatize the power of Black people as a reliable voting bloc. A graduate of Dr. King's alma mater, the event's organizer enjoyed a reputation as a community leader committed to social justice and the arts. At this meeting, he expressed his discontent with Black faith leaders who were not doing enough to enhance the living conditions of Black people within their communities. He criticized local Democratic leaders and what he saw as an uncritical loyalty that Black people demonstrated to the party, which he suggested was to Black people's detriment. Surrounded by Black preachers, he then, with some reservation, disclosed that he voted for Donald Trump in 2016. When pressed, the organizer explained that he believed Trump was best equipped to improve the economic conditions of Black people. My friend pointed out what seemed obvious to the other pastors: "Dude, you voted for a racist? That can't align with your commitment to racial justice."

The leader rebuffed the assertion that race and racism were factors to consider in the 2020 presidential election. He spoke adamantly to an overdue need for Black voters to consider class and vote their way into wealth, leaving behind what conservatives regularly call "the party of handouts." He supported this claim by mentioning how well his 401(k) did under the Trump administration. The pastor downplayed the ongoing role of race in charting paths for millions of people into poverty and political sterility.

This Black pastor bought into the notion that economic justice competes with racial justice instead of holding the two side by side. Yet true human liberation requires that we diligently hold the complexities of power relations and identity side by side, resisting the temptation to rank oppressions and deny hardships. The intersectional nature of oppression is what Patricia Hill Collins terms "a matrix of domination."[1] Dismantling one form of oppression should never distract from an awareness of other forms of oppression. Abolitionist vigor wants to eradicate all forms of oppression.

White noise tells us to compare oppressions, segregating one group from another and quashing any hope for a multiracial justice movement. White people's allegations of equal hardships displace the important role race plays and fuel the oppression olympics. Comparing social suffering is a tactic for changing the subject or introducing such topics as the so-called reverse racism of affirmative action, Black intraracial discrimination, Black-on-Black crime, or the classism cover-up, which relegates racism to a form of oppression less significant than and utterly independent of economic injustice.

Classism does not trump racism. Racism does not trump classism. Sexism does not trump homophobia. We consume and communicate the lies of social constructions crafted to convince us of our places in society. White noise renders us tone-deaf to the pains that stitch us together beyond the fault lines of racial difference. Reparative intercession amplifies commitment to all others and defies all subjugation, understanding that many live at the intersection of various oppressions where systems of domination crisscross the human experience.

As I have seen in my work, racial capitalism proceeds as an ideal foil for exposing the most consequential intersection of racism and classism. Racial capitalism drives wealth in one direction, to the top, trapping poor people in poverty and discarding the majority to compete for resources—a unique legacy of our slavocracy. Racism marches in single file with capitalism. Chattel slavery married racism and capitalism under the open heavens of America, and these resilient bedfellows continue to renew their vows in the sanctuaries of our courts, classrooms, hospitals, and churches each generation.

When white noise dupes us into comparing injustices and fragmenting our calls for justice, we must practice a third rhythm of reparative intercession, pattern recognition, which is about accepting our interdependence and the mutual becoming of all creation woven together into a single garment of destiny.

Pattern recognition quiets the embittering white noise "I've had it hard too, but I worked hard." Race violently intersects with economics, which gives racism its bite and amplifies the myriad ways white noise tells us that Black social immobility is only a product of apathy and a pitiable work ethic. Repairing racial harm requires recognizing patterns of interlocking inequalities. This way of knowing and being appreciates our interdependence and shared futures instead of seeing us as divested from and in ferocious competition with the good of the whole. In a dank Birmingham jail, Dr. King jotted down on the edges of a newspaper, "Injustice anywhere is a threat to justice everywhere. We are caught in an inescapable network of mutuality, tied in a single garment of destiny. Whatever affects one directly, affects all indirectly."[2] Recognizing patterns of oppression, which stir a brutal competitiveness at the intersection of race and class, mandates a new way of relating to each other: persistent neighborliness.

Before the Skin Issue Was a "Sin" Issue

As we covered in chapter 1, elite groups of White men socially and religiously constructed a power structure that systemically and systematically distributes opportunities and obstructions according to race. White noise tells us that these opportunities and obstructions, these affirmations and negations, are natural and inevitable. We say, "It's just the way things are." Whiteness reinvents its symbols, practices, and meaning to defend power and wealth. Whiteness draws on whatever it needs to keep predatory history alive and felt as natural.

Borrowing a notion from Cedric Robinson, I suggest that racial capitalism refuses to unknot the dynamics of race and class.[3] Racial meaning lives in our economy—in healthcare, housing, jobs, banking, and education. Racism loses its teeth without laws and economics that facilitate it. Avoiding the class trap means acknowledging that our country reorganizes economic processes, politics, and social mobility in ways that benefit the richest White people again and again. Consider the tax system of the three-fifths compromise[4] and the 2017 Trump tax law,[5] both of which privileged the White elite, as examples of this reorganization. Capitalism uses race as a tool of its self-perpetuation. In the words of Stewart Hall, "Race is a modality where class lives."[6] Race lives in class, and class lives in race.

White people are victims of oppression too, living under the weight of class, gender, and sex discrimination for more than four hundred years. Prior to the invention of race-based slavery according to skin color, Europeans dominated other Europeans in the interest of expanding master classes of people. Europe "colonized" itself along the lines of race. Europeans prefigured racial differences along the regional, subcultural, and dialectical distinctions of other Europeans—those whom we now call White people. Robinson helped me to see that racism doesn't always depend on differences in skin color. At a minimum, the European beneficiaries of race, who laid the conceptual and violent foundations of the United States, used biological arguments for the legal and economic subjugation of other people living with White skin.

Racialization within Europe propelled the process of colonial invasion, settlement, expropriation, and racial hierarchy. Robinson quotes Louis Leo Snyder, an American scholar of European political history, "Racialists, not satisfied with merely proclaiming the superiority of the white over the coloured race, also felt it necessary to erect a hierarchy within the white race itself." He goes on to say, "To meet this need they developed the myth of the Aryan, or Nordic, superiority. The Aryan myth in turn became the source of other secondary myths such as Teutonism (Germany), Anglo-Saxonism (England and the United States), and Celticism (France)."[7] Not all Europeans inherited this claim to racial superiority. As Robin D. G. Kelley notes, "The first European proletarians were racial subjects (Irish, Jews, Roma or Gypsies, Slavs, etc.) and they were victims of dispossession (enclosure), colonialism, and slavery within Europe."[8] This history draws the distinction between Whiteness as a doctrine and White people.

The egalitarian ideal at the heart of our nation caves under divisive politics meant to nurture and sustain a cardinal feature of Whiteness: domination. The land of the free, our shining beacon on a hill, is a racial-capitalist society owing its emergence and expansion to the violent extraction of natural and human resources through slavery, imperialism, genocide, and war, all of which preyed on White people too. In this same context, the resource-grabbing and labor-exploiting bourgeoisie emerged from particular ethnic and cultural groups; the proletariats of places like England, France, and Germany emerged from other ethnic and cultural groups; the peasants belonged to even more inferior ethnic and cultural groups. Enslaved persons were almost entirely the most inferior in the pecking order. European civilization tended to differentiate, not homogenize.[9] While one might be tempted to see this as a purely economic interpretation of a social hierarchy, it merits repeating that these class distinctions were framed as biological and natural.

By racializing Irish industrial and agricultural workers, the state and the privileged classes could accrue political power and wealth through exploitation. Both the English elite and the working class harbored racist feelings toward the people of Ireland. The anti-Irish orientations of English workers emanated from negative perceptions that Irish immigrants were "stealing the jobs" and depressing wages. This shared disdain for Irish laborers across classes only hardened the resolve to colonize, persecute, and alienate them.[10]

After a while, immigrants from all over Europe used White skin to cash in on the myth of Anglo-Saxonism. "Identifying as White," according to Kelly Brown Douglas, "was the way they negotiated their 'real life context and social experience,' which was riddled with contradictions, most notably in their relationship with the black community."[11] Although some European immigrants pilgrimed from "inferior" parts of Europe—namely, eastern and southern Europe—they could boast their superiority to Blacks and Native Americans due to "the cherished property"[12] of White skin. Whiteness became a passport into civil society, an economic asset, and the body politic of American life. Seeing Blacks as "other" and inferior solidified Whites as a unified class of people in the United States, notwithstanding clear economic and cultural distinctions.

Prior to this realignment, White identity was not exclusively or necessarily about White skin. America, not Europe, invented a unified notion of Whiteness to protect the power, interests, and property of the White elite. This Whiteness, inherited by nearly all light-skinned people of European descent, was constructed against the otherness of Blacks and Native Americans. A limited definition and assumption of Whiteness as an identity category bloomed in the cultural and political soil of America. The expansion of Whiteness to poor Whites and the previously denigrated European immigrant groups protects capitalism by creating competitive divisions between the multiracial working class and middle class. Instead of addressing the ills of capitalism, white laboring classes see non-White people as a threat to their self-interests and embrace the idea of social mobility—a belief they could achieve their aspirations of becoming their exploiters. All the while, the exploitative White elite, which controls most of the wealth and political power, benefit from their labor.

Saving Capitalism: Green, Black, and White

The major world religions, including Christianity, foreground a type of sacredness in humanity. We find God in the face of the other. Human bodies, being, and life are sacred. But the market economy converts the sacred into commodities—lifeless, soulless, transferable objects. Capitalism reduces human life to numbers and dollar signs. For the overwhelming majority of Americans, social mobility appears increasingly fictive, as the status of the middle class becomes staunchly replaced by living paycheck to paycheck. Only a handful of White Americans possess the lion's share of the money and power. Most of us say nothing about wealth inequality, notwithstanding its racial dynamics, because we want to be in the top wealth percentile.

Some years ago, I joined a conference call hosted by the New Jersey Poor People's Campaign. On these calls, the multiracial, multifaith coalition planned a series of civil disobedience actions at the New Jersey State House, where we expected to be arrested and jailed during our protest advocating for legal system reform, education equity, livable wages, and the like. As the first hour passed, we endeavored to list some key guidelines necessary to enact Dr. King's vision for the last campaign he organized before his assassination.

In the middle of the call, a minister from Appalachia expressed dismay over the use of the phrase "poor White folks." Puzzled, the principal on the call halted the agenda and asked the man to explain his concerns. "I grew up in poverty in West Virginia. You don't need to tell me about poverty," he remarked.

"It's the Poor People's Campaign. Dr. King envisioned an intentionally multiracial movement centered on the question of economic disparities. How can we do that without talking about White poverty?" I asked.

The Appalachian native explained, "Every time I hear 'poor White folks,' I hear 'poor White trash.' That's what they called us. That's what White people called me." For him, White poverty exposed the scam of Whiteness as a unified racial identity and challenged a sense of American belonging and human worth. While he thrived in circles for racial justice, the conversation became an abhorrent reminder that White capitalism othered him too.

In his book *Twelve Million Black Voices*, the late Richard Wright states, "The Lords of the Land will preach the doctrine of 'white supremacy' to the poor whites who are eager to form mobs. In the midst of general hysteria, they will seize one of us—it does not matter who, the innocent or the guilty—and, as a token, a naked and bleeding body will be dragged through the dusty streets."[13] Racial capitalism peddles the myth of "hard work alone" and pits the working class against the middle class along the lines of race.

For W. E. B. Du Bois, "The theory of laboring class unity rests upon the assumption that laborers, despite internal jealousies, will unite because of their opposition to the exploitation of the capitalists." White plantation owners and former enslavers roped poor White people into a political alliance that ultimately dashed the promise of Reconstruction, giving vitality to the Southern Redemption. Du Bois continues:

It must be remembered that the white group of laborers, while they received a low wage, were compensated in part by a sort of public and psychological wage. They were given public deference and titles of courtesy because they were white. They were admitted freely with all classes of white people to public functions, public parks, and the best schools. The police were drawn from their ranks, and the courts, dependent on their votes, treated them with such leniency as to encourage lawlessness. Their vote selected public officials, and while this had small effect upon the economic situation, it had great effect upon their personal treatment and the deference shown them.[14]

This allowance spawned policies that merely enriched the coffers and expanded the political interests of the plantation class, not the labor class of White folks.

Calling Whiteness a psychological wage in no way negates the tangible dividends of White privilege that working-class White people unconsciously enjoy. White identity generally means their families have greater access to healthcare. White skin minimizes the chances that a young man will be gunned down by a police officer. White identity increases the likelihood of higher wages and better employment opportunities. White skin prevents serial surveillance in retail stores. Whiteness, for the better part of US history, has meant unquestioned and unencumbered access to the ballot box. White skin allows a person to live anyplace their finances can afford without facing neighbor flight, real estate agent biases, and bank discriminations. These unearned advantages notwithstanding, the majority of White people experience forms of exploitation and exclusion suited to capitalism by the infinitesimal class of White rulers—the persons at the largely unfathomable apex of our racial hierarchy.

The wages of Whiteness do transcend the psychological and immaterial. It is important to mention that Black and Brown families occupy the slippery lower rungs of the middle class, just a traumatic life event or two from poverty. Between 2007 and 2013, White middle-income families saw a 31 percent decrease in median wealth to $131,900. Their Black counterparts, during that same period, saw a decrease of 47 percent, falling to $33,600.[15] Tax law professor Dorothy Brown avers, "A Black household with the same income as a white household is statistically more likely to need two working spouses to earn that amount, to have less home equity, and to be supporting family members who were overtly and legally prohibited from the same wealth-building opportunities available to the family members of white workers."[16] In order to minimize the demoralizing impact of Trump's policies, many pointed to "record low unemployment" among Black Americans prior to the COVID-19 pandemic shutdown. This distortion of "the numbers," which is white noise, flouts that many of these jobs remain low-wage gigs that fail to alter the racial wealth and income gaps. In fact, these low-income jobs proliferate racial inequality and drain wealth out of Black homes. Poverty-level wages rarely result in homeownership, sustainable savings, and discretionary funds for investing—if they even cover the monthly living expenses. Poverty corresponds to higher divorce rates, sicknesses, and family dislocation and instability.

White and Black households with equivalent incomes do not currently pay the same amount in federal taxes.[17] Black families pay more than White families. In *The Whiteness of Wealth*, Brown says, "Taxpayers in the highest income zip codes have historically claimed the most deductions, while taxpayers in the lower-income zip codes typically take only the standard deductions."[18] Poor people, in general, fare badly against a tax system that privileges the rich. The government requires Black people to pay into a tax system that refuses to protect their rights and lives. In fact, Black bodies were tax incentives for elite Whites when they were property.

Nonetheless, many White working-class people are reluctant to see Black and Brown working-class people as allies in toppling an economic organization that feasts on them all. This is the class trap. White privilege masks the White elite as the perpetrators of economic injustice and scapegoats Brown immigrants for White job loss and Black people for monopolizing public benefits and cheating the system. White noise blames equally positioned Black and Brown folks for White wage depression, White college admission denials, and White job insecurity. This is why Otis Madison opined that the purpose of racism is to control the actions of White people, not Black people.[19]

During the 2008 presidential campaign, race figured prominently in public discourse and political strategies on the right and the left for the first time in my adult life. The sin of Whiteness—which worships itself, demonizes the other, and separates us through segregation—deployed working-class and middle-class White men and women to protect America from any misalignment with their values. The idea of a Black man vying for the White House drew armed White men out of their caves of racial resentment to defend a way of life that virtually amounted to self-sabotage.

My spiritual mom, Dr. Martha Simmons, ordered her first subscription to cable after witnessing groups of White people with guns protest outside rallies hosted by the Obama campaign. Seared into her memory are the voices of Black community elders rehearsing, "'They' are going to kill that boy before election day." My memi told me in hushed tones, "Some rednecks will kill him if he wins. . . . I remember when 'they' killed Martin."

These White folks who were angered by Obama's presidential run lived more outside the boundaries of the White power structure than the Black man they figured they could intimidate. From those carrying loaded firearms, to those in the Tea Party, to those promoting the birther conspiracy, to those who voted for Trump, segments of America pine for a country that sees them, honors them, and represents them. Every citizen and resident of a nation deserves this consideration from their leaders as the bare minimum and norm. However, they miscalculate the source of their displacement and distress. After four hundred years under the rule of White plutocrats, many Whites have ended up without property, education, or a secure way to provide for themselves and their families.

The One Percent Ain't Us

Indeed, White noise blames victims of economic injustice instead of their oppressors. Here are some plain and unattractive truths: the top 1 percent of Americans own 40 percent of the country's wealth and 90 percent of its income.[20] The wealthiest 400 Americans own more than the 150 million adults in the bottom 60 percent of our racialized wealth pyramid.[21] Gearing up for the 2020 race for the Oval Office, Senator Elizabeth Warren, herself a millionaire, tweeted an even more unattractive truth: "The top 0.1 percent, who'd pay my #UltraMillionaireTax, own about the same wealth as 90 percent of America."[22]

According to a joint study by Americans for Tax Fairness and by Inequality.org, billionaires' wealth grew by $1.6 trillion (55 percent) during the first thirteen months of the COVID-19 pandemic in the United States. As 70 million jobs and 600,000 lives disappeared, the pandemic became just another context for the superrich to become richer. The study approximates that this increase represents one-third of all wealth gains over a thirty-one-year period, from 1990 to 2021. With $4.56 trillion, the 719 US billionaires own over four times more wealth than the combined $1.01 trillion belonging to the nearly 165 million Americans in the bottom half of the nation's economic life.[23] Contrary to public perceptions, many White people lacked $400 in savings and waited in long food pantry lines as COVID-19 froze our economy.

When adjusted for inflation, the average income in the country has remained approximately the same for the last forty years. By comparison, over the last two decades, the richest Americans have seen their income triple, relative to that of the poorest Americans. During the economic expansion of the Clinton years, the top

1 percent relished in a 98.7 percent jump in income, while the rest of us—though I was not even in high school—saw only a 20 percent hike in income during what we tenderly remember as a time of great surplus. Under Clinton, colloquially lauded as the first Black president in many Black communities, the one-percenters possessed 45 percent of the growth in income.[24]

The share of American adults who live in middle-income households decreased from 61 percent in 1971 to 51 percent in 2019. From 2009 through 2012, what the expert class refers to as the Great Recession's recovery period, the vultures at the top captured 95 percent of all income, leaving the other 99 percent of us 5 percent, despite the greed-deranged role the superrich played in bankrupting the nation in the first place.[25] For the top 5 percent, their median net worth increased by 4 percent, to $4.8 million from 2007 to 2016. In contrast, the net worth of families in the lower tiers of wealth decreased by at least 20 percent during the same years.[26]

In reality, working-class White people have more in common with equally situated Black and Brown people than they do with the rich White people so many of us long to be. White privilege disallows poor and working-class White people from seeing the White corporate class as the assailant on their upward mobility and household sustainability. White noise fosters White racial resentment based on an illusion that non-White people are replacing White people. This lie presses vast groups of middle-income White people to see themselves as victims of the preferential treatment of "undeserving" Black and Brown people. The pus-filled sores of racial resentment enable the spread of this deadly infection.

Politicians exploit these resentments. White noise causes some to vote against programs that would benefit the poor, such as healthcare reform, food security policies, tax hikes on the rich, gun reform, education funding, and green jobs. White noise makes us forget that working-class White folks have also experienced voter suppression in the South.[27] As Black Lives Matter, the organizing slogan of the eponymous movement, unnerves and agitates White

America, I am moved to ask, Do all White lives matter to White people? It seems White privilege, power, and superiority matter more than actual White lives.

Shrinking wealth and savings, dead-end jobs that cause one to live hand to mouth, growing substance dependence, and a swelling inability to guarantee a better life for their kids cause many White people to think they don't have privilege and power. By nature of their relationship to Whiteness, they still fare better in terms of education, healthcare, and political access than the vast majority of Brown and Black people. However, the social pain experienced by middle-class White families is real. But Black and Latinx people are not to blame. The privileged few receive a pass for the ongoing extraction of resources and exploitation of labor in the name of high profits. While White people are angry at Black workers and Latinx immigrants for disappearing jobs and diminishing wages, the true culprits of their economic conditions are the superrich. The real economic danger faced by working-class White people is intra-White exploitation—White-on-White discrimination.

Won't You Be My Neighbor?

Pattern recognition traces the ways race and class, among other social constructs, intersect in the lives of people anxiously and impatiently struggling to navigate public life. White noise induces untenable interracial competition on both sides of Whiteness, which reflects a predatory rivalry on one side and a deprecating competitiveness on the other. The rhythm of pattern recognition reaches for an alternative way of showing up in racist space, an unorthodox approach to human flourishing amid the aggressive disinheritance wrought by White privilege and power. Despite difference and the divisions driven by competition, no person lives "outside the magnetic field of ethical concern"[28] when we take up the call to persistent neighborliness. Persistent neighborliness is a quality of community anchored in interdependence and mutual becoming. How do we wrest free of bootstrap thinking, racial competition, and greed?

Howard Thurman states, "Once the neighbor is defined, then one's moral obligation is clear. . . . Every [person] is potentially every other [person's] neighbor." He goes on to assert, "Neighborliness is nonspatial; it is qualitative. A [person] must love his neighbor directly, clearly, permitting no barriers between."[29] Though we lack an organic and deliberate facility for neighborliness, the entire globe is our neighborhood. Persistent neighborliness is a reorientation to life. It happens when we see that "the same things that work in me on behalf of my own preservation become operative now in me with regard to the other-than-myself that has been included in this extension of myself."[30] We remove competition when we affirm that our lowest common denominator is one of our highest ideals: irreducible humanness.

Persistent neighborliness is a skill, a discipline, requiring a new way of community. Ben Witherington summarizes the call to neighborliness via Jesus's parable about the self-sacrificing Samaritan: "Jesus proclaimed a radical ethic that had as its central tenet love of God and neighbor, even if that neighbor happened to be a hated enemy."[31] We disrupt racial individualism, divisiveness, and competition through this radical practice of neighborliness. "The fine art of neighborliness"[32] compels us to commit to memory through our daily behaviors and interactions an irreducible awareness of our mutuality and interdependence, even under the most unequal circumstances and extreme racist pressure.

Thurman cautioned us in the 1960s to wake up to this truth because our window of time for self-correction is closing. Our time is running out to save democracy and, more urgently, the planet from the injurious competition that maintains racial hierarchy, the silencing of racial truth-telling (parrhesia), and gross inaction. There is only one way to reverse the hope-distorting, people-devouring patterns of racial capitalism upheld by the white noise of fixation on a work ethic. As a multiracial movement seeking to redress the Whiteness in our wealth, income, hiring practices, and tax system, we name the carnivorous design of our economy, which devours all those on the bottom regardless of the color of their skin, and the narratives of difference that guide us. This posture of togetherness anticipates opposition and resolves to advance altruistic and reparative opportunities.

Persistent neighborliness purges bootstrap theology, which was birthed from the myth of meritocracy and the Protestant work ethic and conveys that "God helps those who help themselves." Bootstrap theology simultaneously sanctifies hard work and veils mass discrimination along the lines of race. After 246 years as unpaid slave laborers and more than a century and a half of racial capitalism, Black people can overwork in multiple jobs, earn "triple time," graduate from Howard University, and still scarcely manage to make ends meet month to month. Yet white noise says that Black economic disparities result from laziness, apathy, or imprudence. Bootstrap theology ascribes upward mobility to hard work. While only a handful of White people possess the majority of the money, the smokescreen of meritocracy makes the superrich seem "just successful" and hardworking and this obscures the ways the rules are rigged in their favor.

Sharing Is Subversive

Neighborliness shares out of its abundance or scarcity as an act of resistance. A multiracial coalition of generous resource sharing can weaken the commodifying and totalizing powers of racial capitalism. The socioeconomic and political crises incarnated in gang and drug cultures, massive levels of gun violence and opioid addictions in White working-class communities, climbing suicide rates and political failures, unsustainable unemployment levels, and unsatisfactory public education all demand persistent neighborliness.

I draw again from an ancient source of wisdom to add texture to neighborliness. The New Testament invites us to visualize the power of human sharing following the Pentecost episode.

When the day of Pentecost had come, they were all together in one place. And suddenly from heaven there came a sound like the rush of a violent wind, and it filled the entire house where they were sitting. Divided tongues, as of fire, appeared among them, and a tongue rested on each of them. All of them were filled with the Holy Spirit and began to speak in other languages, as the Spirit gave them ability. Now there were devout Jews from every nation under heaven living in Jerusalem. And at this sound the crowd gathered and was bewildered, because each one heard them speaking in the native language of each. . . . Awe came upon everyone, because many wonders and signs were being done by the apostles. All who believed were together and had all things in common; they would sell their possessions and goods and distribute the proceeds to all, as any had need. (Acts 2:1–6, 43–45)

The author of Acts introduces the economic arrangement of the first-century house churches, *ekklēsia*—pooling all resources in common and meeting the needs of all—after the advent of Pentecost. The egalitarian and economic ethics of the *ekklēsia* derive from a shared and transferable experience of equal access to the Spirit. Persistent neighborliness calls us to intercede on behalf of the most vulnerable and to bolster the true power of these unprotected peoples. The economic life of the early Jesus movement echoes again in Acts 4:

Now the whole group of those who believed were of one heart and soul, and no one claimed private ownership of any possessions, but everything they owned was held in common. . . . There was not a needy person among them, for as many as owned lands or houses sold them and brought the proceeds of what was sold. They laid it at the apostles' feet, and it was distributed to each as any had need. (vv. 32, 34–35)

Pentecost economics summons us beyond individual concerns toward a new communal horizon of sufficiency, equity, and justice.

Many people need higher wages; paid medical and family leave; affordable, quality healthcare; and better funded public schools.

Persistent neighborliness sees all humans as Spirit people. Spirit people is a way of referring to humanity—beings created in the image of God, enlivened by the breath of God, and carrying a spark of divinity. Persistent neighborliness transcends social constructs used to create hierarchies, validate power distribution, and maintain social control. Persistent neighborliness recognizes that we all walk this road paved by White supremacy and amplifies our ethical obligation to do something reparative, even if it heals the material and interior lives of only one other person.

Pooling resources is a subversive act in a racial-capitalist society. Walter Brueggemann posits, "Justice is the maintenance of neighborliness that permits all members of the community to flourish without the distortion or subversion of economic leverage."[33] Persistent neighborliness operates in and on behalf of the margins. As demonstrated at Pentecost, this solidarity transcends language barriers, ethnic/racial identity, gender binaries, and religious commitments to ensure that every household's needs are met. As we advocate for anti-racist, anti-capitalist policies to transform our economy, we can collectively practice neighborliness that reaches everyone. Until wealth flows in all directions, we must see ourselves as responsible for each other.

Persistent neighborliness practices the presence of God in its commitment to target human need and to operate in the margins. The multiethnic, multiclass, multigender, multilingual character of the Spirit community that crosses the boundaries of social competition, resentment, misunderstanding, and distrust is transferrable and translatable. While pooling resources may sound like an unattractive and impractical ideal, we can stand up to corporate vultures feasting on our divisions and address the widening economic divide through resource-sharing, collective economics, and a multiracial coalition that creates a greater sense of belonging and mutuality.

Embracing Our Complementariness

Persistent neighborliness abandons all ranks and considers it "bad manners" to formulate differentiations for the purposes of demeaning, dislocating, disinheriting, and dominating. The heart of interdependence beats around the embrace of radical mutuality. Many indigenous communities instinctively practiced neighborliness prior to the cultural disruptions and impositions of colonial power.

To be true to my own spiritual formation, it feels right to turn to the wisdom of an African people tradition. (To talk of Africa as a singular place, people, and culture is an invention of Whiteness and white noise that obliterates the diversity of the continent and the historical and prehistoric significance those peoples had in the evolution of human civilization.) The Tonga people of Zambia and Zimbabwe modeled a social structure that privileged every voice equally. No single element of social organization predominated in their internal social arrangement. At the core of this native democratic culture was a moral philosophy that valued interdependence—that is, relationships to one another, ancestors, creation, the unborn, and life itself.

The *mukowa*—an extended network of kinship, accountability, and mutual aid—represented the greatest unit of organization in Tonga communities. Family was a porous concept. In *Terms of Order*, Cedric Robinson says of the Tonga society, "Any individual who can establish a claim of any kind to a member of the *mukowa*, can be absorbed and treated as if he or she were a close relative. . . . A man establishes this claim by practical activity, such as helping at funerals, contributing to the marriage-payments made by men of the *mukowa*, helping pay fines and damages—and in the end he will be helped in turn."[34] The other fills out our sense of family, uncovers our blindspots, gives different meaning to our lives, and shares in our oppressions and overcoming.

The Tonga offer a vivid picture of the real possibility for a people to produce a society without the need for rulers and a hierarchy.

For these African peoples, the principle of incompleteness speaks to the complementary character of life. We are all equally incomplete in search of each other. Power, domination, and hierarchy are circumvented by the will and the need to remain one with all.[35] We need what is external to us to fully achieve ourselves. This subverts White power and privilege.

Simply opening our hearts to the other is not enough to eradicate the racial competition and resentment we endure. We must see God in the face of the other as they are and respond out of thorough, nonnegotiable siblinghood—"a metaphysics of kinship"[36] that wakes with us every morning. With a disposition of universal sisterhood and brotherhood, we can hold the creative tension of our differences and still see our futures wedded as one.

Persistent neighborliness improves our relationships across the lines of dissimilarity engineered to isolate the haves from the have-nots. Persistent neighborliness looks like identifying resources and time to invest in disinvested communities; using familial language for othered persons—Black sisters, Latinx siblings, or Asian brothers; practicing consumerism in non-White communities and businesses; advocating for residential and school integration; daily journaling about our interdependence on others for subsistence, public safety, healthcare, and education; and remembering others as God's creation.

Persistent neighborliness projects a new way of knowing, a new psychological wage, bankrolled by siblinghood and interdependence, which sponsors our everyday capacity to rearrange our racial situation toward something economically, spiritually, and politically sustainable. This psychological wage rejects the need to feel superior or on top, negating the power of racial hierarchy.

"Why does everything have to be about race?"

4

Syncopated Identity

Exploring Our Fuller Selves

At a recent protest, a White activist told me about a conversation involving her supervisor and coworkers. She said she was particularly disappointed in her boss "Jim." During a staff meeting, Jim said to the team about a Black male employee, "I'm pleasantly surprised Mark turns in his assignments on time. I didn't think you were that guy!" Mark, the only Black man on the team, had been with the organization for only a few months and had no issues with lateness. Pulling Jim aside after the meeting, Mark asserted that Jim's remark included some racist assumptions. The supervisor insisted that he wasn't racist and that his comment had nothing to do with race. However, Jim never explained why he expressed those sentiments or what they meant.

"Other than the boss, I was the only White person in the room," the activist told me. "I felt like it was clear that something needed to be said and that I was the one who should say it, but was I supposed to say it immediately? Wait for a private conversation? Confirm with my Black coworkers first about my choices?" Obviously nervous, she recollected that she said to her boss, "It is not up to you to decide if what you said was racist. Your intention might have been to make a joke, but the impact was negative and harmful to Mark. Impact is what matters, Jim."

In the United States, race figures prominently in our unconscious public interactions. We respond to the phantom of race and expose our implicit biases. We cannot rise above the hum of white noise without looking at microaggressions. Derald Wing Sue, a psychologist and expert on multicultural counseling, defines microaggressions as "the everyday slights, insults, indignities, and invalidations delivered toward people of color because of their visible racial/ethnic minority characteristics."[1] The term potentially trivializes these behaviors, but nothing small occurs when non-White people endure these disempowering interactions.

Microaggressions reveal our implicit biases—the unconscious and involuntary attitudes toward a person's or a group's identity. We all develop these feelings over time through overt and concealed messages we encounter daily. These impulsive reactions to people based on race can harm the emotional, mental, and physical well-being of persons on the receiving end. The "micro" in microaggression communicates the interpersonal, individual character of the behavior, not the scope and impact of the trauma. Microaggressive speech and action benefit from white noise, because white noise convinces us that the words or actions are harmless. White noise tells us, "I/they did not mean it, so it's okay."

Microaggressions cause many non-White people to be self-conscious about what they wear, the volume of their voice, their dialect, and their response to racism. I often internalize my feeble attempts to avoid experiencing racial microaggressions as humiliating. Even when I am not the perpetrator, I still walk away owning the problem as if I did something wrong. Many non-White people walk away from a racist encounter internalizing the message behind the clutched purse or the disparaging question or the comment about their "exceptionalness" into their conceptions of self.

From childhood into senior adulthood, we are *shaped* by the iniquity of message-giving and meaning-setting systems of relations. We are told lies about who we are and how we are supposed to behave. Our perceptual sins, which inhabit our behavioral sins, find formation in the following contexts:

- family
- church
- media
- literature

- friends
- school
- architecture
- social media

These message-givers and meaning-setters legitimate our negative, unconscious racial thinking.

When white noise rings out in our self-conceptions and perceptions of the other, a fourth rhythm of reparative intercession, syncopated identity, presents us with an opportunity to interrogate the fullness of our identities. It is not enough to pore over the specific behaviors we must avoid; we must preemptively pursue new attitudes and actions that promote mutuality and interdependence. A syncopated identity compels us to own our racial identity out loud and courageously pursue cross-racial contact instead of asking, "Why does everything have to be about race?" Achieving a syncopated identity allows people to see themselves as multidimensional individuals who seek to encounter the other—who also are multidimensional individuals—in ways that are reparative, not predatory or apathetic. This way of being a conscious self is an attitudinal and behavioral adjustment that involves self-confession, body talk, and storying the self.

Self-Confession: The Sins Ever Before Us

A syncopated identity allows us to get to know the unflattering truth of our biases. Probing and unmasking how we respond to race and its intersection with our identities and those of others is a potentially jarring process. Confessing our racial sin opens up our lives for the personal transformation that must accompany structural change in order for true abolition of racism to have a chance. Per our articulation of White grief, confession is good for the soul and constitutive of reparative intercession. Self-confession involves acknowledging the impact of racial differences, assessing our relationship to power, naming our sin of Whiteness with specificity, and questioning what our actions mean for the promise of how we embody the *imago Dei*.

One of the most unsettling introspective features of the Public Love Organizing and Training (PLOT) curriculum is the Stereotype Dump Exercise (the Dump). Reflecting on twenty or so identity groups, participants traverse the room calling out all the stereotypes, both positive and negative, that come to mind. The exercise is designed to increase participants' awareness of unconscious stereotypes they might have about different identity groups by expressing any and every one that exists in the American imagination. Through self- and group reflection, participants hopefully grow more aware of the potential influence of unconscious biases on their decision-making.

During a retreat with educators in Chicago, Hellen—a White private-school administrator—gave voice to the value of self-confession as we wrapped up the Dump. On poster paper labeled with racial, cultural, and ethnic groups, eighteen attendees wrote down any thoughts related to African Americans, Africans, Whites, Asians, older adults, the formerly incarcerated, women, queer people, Muslims, the wealthy, and more.

Participants unloaded scores of stereotypes before we read them aloud. Once participants were assembled in small groups, robust dialogue steered the room into one of the first discomforting yet transparent moments of our time together. One Black participant said, "When we wrote stereotypes about different groups of people, I was uncomfortable reflecting on the language that described me, my race. We are not criminals . . . or lazy . . . or freeloaders . . .

or hypersexual." Hellen expressed uneasiness when writing down and listening to the assumptions about certain groups. She said passionately, "I was petrified that someone would think that I felt some of the horrible things that were written about African Americans." She confessed, "But I should feel guilty for actually performing these thoughts when I used the elevator instead of the escalator at the mall last weekend because two young Latino guys came up behind me." Her self-confession communicated vulnerability, culpability, and specificity. She named a sin out loud and even looked to the future. She concluded, "I really need to do some things differently. My private thoughts matter. They matter because they are no longer private when I easily do things like this." Self-confession reveals the biases buried under our microaggressions, biases that need our examination so we can confront them.

Microaggressions are daily, individual examples of the sin of Whiteness. White sin elevates Whiteness to the level of the ultimate, demonizes non-White lives and bodies, and segments humanity. Again, Whiteness is idolatrous, demonic, and segregationist. Particularly, White idolatry solemnizes racial hierarchy as natural. We need to confess racist habits and microaggressive behaviors in spite of their unconscious nature.

The lie of racial hierarchy prevents us from knowing the truth about our enculturation into racism. This fallacy dictates how we see, move, and think in private and public. It tells us the demonic, dehumanizing narratives of Black sexual predation, laziness, unintelligence, and violence while veiling the ugly history of Whiteness, which is alive all around us. Endowed with colorful narratives of the threat of Black bodies, we seldom direct our attention to the disgusting and sordid events that make an enemy necessary in order to preserve a belief in our own innocence.

A predominance of our racialized mistrust, myths, and mistreatments springs from our penchant for projections. Projections program White people to roll up their windows and lock their car doors when my Black skin moves too close. Projections motivated a White couple in Center City, Philadelphia, to walk more quickly, although I dragged along at least ten feet behind them. Harvard's campus police routinely requested to see my student ID whenever I left the stacks of Widener Library after midnight, though I never witnessed them take the same precautions with White persons.

Lynching and lynch culture inscribed the malevolent lie of hypersexuality on the skin of Black men while ignoring the four centuries of White men raping non-White women. Black mass criminalization permits us to ignore that White men robbed Africa of land and labor for hundreds of years and stole land and natural resources from indigenous peoples in the Americas, Australia, and Asia. The genocidal colonization of lands we now call the United States, which claimed millions of Black and Native American lives, hides behind the distracting diversion toward "Black-on-Black" violence.

The stinging reach of the doctrine of Whiteness through micro-aggressive behavior demands that we confront said behavior internally and externally. Survivors of microaggressions must internally and immediately reject the messaging underneath them and, when it is deemed safe to their physical health, must redirect the encounter with open-ended questions and corrective comments. Table 4.1 is informed and inspired by Derald Wing Sue and colleagues to help us identify and unpack racial microaggressions as sin to which we can respond.

Table 4.1. Examples of Racial Microaggressions

Theme	Microaggression	Message	White Sin	Responses*
Alien in One's Own Land	"Where are you from? No, like where are you really from?"	You are not American.	Sin as segregation—denies belonging and place.	"I said from Texas. Why is that hard to believe?"

Theme	Microaggression	Message	White Sin	Responses*
Ascription of Intelligence	"You are so articulate."	Black and Brown people are generally not as intelligent as White people.	Sin as idolatry—affirms the racial hierarchy and denies the universality of the *imago Dei*.	"Do you mean articulate for a Black person?" "Why do you sound surprised?"
Colorblindness	"When I look at you, I don't see color."	A person's racial experiences are not legitimate.	Sin as idolatry—invalidates a person's unique experiences and right to be heard while affirming White experience as the universal experience.	"I see a White person when I see you. Is there something wrong with my color?" "Are you saying my experiences as a Black person are not real?"
Assumptions of Criminality	A White person calls the local police to report a Black person jogging through the neighborhood.	A non-White person is dangerous and out of place.	Sin as demonic—criminalizes Black bodies, which is a form of dehumanization, and denies the universality of the *imago Dei* within Black people.	"This is my community. Black people live in this community too." "What you are doing is racist." "I have a right to run, shop, study, eat, walk, and drive while Black."
Denial of Individual Racism	"As a gay man, I know what you go through as a Latinx person."	Your racial oppression is no different from my oppression as a gay person. "I cannot be racist. I'm like you."	Sin as idolatry—invalidates the nuances of racial oppression and upholds mythic innocence.	"You actually do not know what it is like to be a Latinx person, and I do not know how difficult it is to be White and gay."

Theme	Microaggression	Message	White Sin	Responses*
Myth of Meritocracy	"How'd your daughter get into Harvard?"	Black and Latinx people are given unfair benefits due to their race.	Sin as segregation—communicates that some non-White communities do not belong in certain spheres of power and denies equal or greater work of said communities.	"Do Black students not attend Ivy League schools? Have you not met any smart Black people?"
Pathologizing Cultural Values / Communication Styles	Asking a Black person, "Why do you have to be so loud? Just speak normally."	Non-White people should assimilate to the dominant culture.	Sin as demonic—problematizes a person's emotional truths and projects a desire for sameness, a form of controlling the other.	"There is nothing wrong with my tone." "That is a tool of control." "I am entitled to my feelings and a constructive way to express them."
Second-Class Citizen	A maître d' seats a group of White diners before a group of Black diners, although the Black group arrived first.	White people are more valued customers than non-White people.	Sin as segregation—assumes White people belong in an establishment because they tip better or make for a better serving experience.	"Excuse me. We were here first." "I need to speak to a manager about my experience." "I will be reporting this experience to the Better Business Bureau."

Theme	Microaggression	Message	White Sin	Responses*
Environmental Microaggressions	Public schools in Black and Brown communities experience overcrowding and underfunding.	People of color don't/ shouldn't value education.	Sin as segregation— underscores the racial power differential and assumes Black and Latinx communities deserve under-performing, substandard ac-commodations.	Advocate for changes as an individual, join a preexisting or new coali-tion, and/or use nonviolent direct action.

Adapted from Derald Wing Sue, Christina Capodilupo, Gina Torino, Jennifer Buc-ceri, Aiasha Holder, Kevin Nadal, and Marta Esquilin, "Racial Microaggressions in Everyday Life: Implications for Clinical Practice," *American Psychologist* 62, no. 4 (2007): 271–86.

* Judgment regarding the safety of responding in any given situation should always be taken into account.

A PLOT participant recounted a racial microaggression while at work:

I was running a staff meeting when I worked for one company. At that point, I had been with the company for five or six years but was new to this department. In addition to being one of the youngest on staff, I was one of only two Black women in this department—the only Afro-Latina. The rest of the team was White. At the con-clusion of the meeting, one of my coworkers asked me where I lived. When I told him, his eyes got wide, and he asked a series of questions without waiting for responses: "Is it safe there? Can you walk down the streets in that area? That seems like a rough neighborhood. Is it hard for you to live there? How many buses and trains do you have to take?"

I decided to make my responses semi-sarcastic and semi-educational. I said, "My neighborhood is no less safe than your neighborhood. Why do you think it's a rough neighborhood? Why wouldn't I be able to walk down the street? I drive my Audi to work, so no trains or buses." I then reminded him that the Boston marathon bomber was found a couple of streets over from our office building. So any neighborhood could be unsafe at any given time.

The coworker expressed an interest in the woman's personal life and well-being, but his microaggression served as a mask for his implicit racial bias.

Practice, Practice

Racial inequality hinges on structures and individual practices working in concert in ways that benefit White people. If we focus solely on the individual's role in maintaining racial inequities, we obscure how our politics, economy, legal system, and schools enforce White supremacy. The structural, invisible hands and feet of racism matter for any serious deliberation on race, bias, and power. However, to situate racism only in the realm of the structural is to miss the daily practices of employers, cops, politicians, parents, doctors, and partners that perpetuate the problems. Individuals matter too for dialing up corrective action to address the harm.

Imani Perry writes:

> People engage in practices of racial inequality in a wide range of contexts, including individual, interactive, collaborative, and administrative decision making. Often it boils down to choices made in the context of asymmetric power relations, where one party must choose how to distribute resources or opportunities that impact others. In contexts such as employment, health care, education, law enforcement, housing, and more, the evidence demonstrates that, in the aggregate, people make choices that tend to advantage Whites.[2]

We swear by common rationales that justify inequality:

- I just want to live in safe neighborhoods.
- I just want my kids to go to the best schools.

- I don't want my property value depreciated.
- I just think people should work for everything they get.
- I don't want my grandchildren loaded down by the national debt.

According to Perry, "The accumulation of practices of inequality—engaged in by professionals, average citizens, and residents, as well as by groups acting in a common interest—translates to large-scale institutional, social, economic, and political inequalities."[3] Hiring inequity, residential and school segregation, and bad public policy receive oxygen from narratives we harbor and tell that do not require the mention of race.

White employers preserve White privilege when they disproportionately hire and promote White people. White admissions personnel feed White privilege by accepting White students into baccalaureate programs ahead of non-Whites of equal or superior ability. White voters uphold White privilege by supporting politicians striving to limit voting rights to secure their political careers. White homeowners embed themselves in White privilege when they flee from diversifying blocks and form unofficial community associations that curate their neighbors. Even good-hearted White people invest in White privilege.

That Sounds about White

According to a 2019 Pew research study, more than two-thirds of Asian and Black adults at least sometimes talked about race with family and friends, compared to roughly half of White and Latinx adults.[4] White people directly engaged the topic the least of all racial groups. However, we talk about race more than we often acknowledge; we simply stash our race-talk behind more obtuse buzzwords. From politics to pulpits, we have developed a vernacular for evoking racial images and racist impact without referencing race. "I just want to live in safe neighborhoods" means Black people bring crime into communities. "I just want my kids to go to the best schools" suggests that predominantly Black and Brown schools are inherently inferior because they are Black and Brown. "I don't want my property value depreciated" communicates a determination to limit the number of Black residents or a resolution to relocate. "I just think people should work for everything they get" infers that non-White people benefit from preferential treatment that adversely impacts hardworking White people. "I don't want my grandchildren loaded down by the national debt" dog whistles how they do not want Blacks and Mexicans living off the taxpayer.

Paul Scully is a middle-aged White man who has had an outsized impact on my work as a community organizer and political thinker. Our paths crossed in spring 2019. More than sixty-six years after *Brown v. Board of Education*, New Jersey is home to the sixth-most segregated public schools in the United States for Black students and the seventh-most for Latinx students.[5] Paul helped me assemble a multiracial coalition of labor leaders, educators, parents, and faith leaders to slay the aged beast of racial isolation and neglect in our public schools. Our interracial, Black-led movement champions the rights of students and families and demands the abolition of education apartheid in our state. Racial and economic segregation in schools impacts the political power, educational outcomes, and economic futures of Black, Latinx, and poor White students.

At the planning meeting for our first town hall and community-education event, leaders around the table were excited about ramping-up turnout and hearing the voices of impacted families. Once Paul announced the meeting would be in Pleasantville, I witnessed concern on the faces of the organizers. One Black labor leader broke the silence, asking, "Do you think people will really come to Pleasantville at that time of night?" A White woman added, "That's a good question. I was concerned just coming tonight." I saw how racist assumptions find their way into racial justice ventures. In a meeting about ending racial segregation, the team questioned if White people would feel safe enough in a Black town victimized by White flight and a middle-class exodus. Even without racial identifiers, we all knew the coded substitutes for race talk. They were talking about race without talking about race.

Talking about race without talking about race is likewise a political tactic that veils racism and presents as race neutral. The law-and-order rhetoric of Richard Nixon's administration cemented the racialization of crime in American public policy. John Ehrlichman, a former Nixon policy advisor, recently exposed the insidious political ploy to recruit the nation's legal system and law enforcement institutions to achieve the administration's conspiracy of Whiteness.

> The Nixon campaign in 1968, and the Nixon White House after that, had two enemies: the antiwar left and black people. You understand what I'm saying? . . . We knew we couldn't make it illegal to be either against the war or black, but by getting the public to associate the hippies with marijuana and blacks with heroin, and then criminalizing both heavily, we could disrupt those communities. We could arrest their leaders, raid their homes, break up their meetings, and vilify them night after night on the evening news. Did we know we were lying about the drugs? Of course we did.[6]

White evangelicals of Billy Graham's era—the Nixon era—hid their law-and-order racism behind the cover of conservative Black leaders like Tom Skinner (early on), Edward Victor Hill, and Howard Jones. Interpreting the impact of Skinner, once known as the Black Billy Graham, historian Aaron Griffith states, "White evangelicals reading his work could be assured not only that the cities were dangerous, crime-ridden places, but also that ghettos, not racism, harbored the most pressing and real danger to black life."[7] However, during Nixon's first term, Skinner fell into disrepute with Graham and the evangelical establishment for excoriating the movement's high-pitched cries for law-and-order as "all the order for [Black communities] and all the law for them. . . . The police in the black community become nothing more than the occupational force present in the black community for the purpose of maintaining the interests of white society."[8] Still, Black ministers like Howard Jones and Edward Victor Hill continued to mask the racism of law-and-order politics during their primetime spot in Graham's densely populated crusades, even while police presence intensified and became increasingly militarized in predominantly Black neighborhoods.

In a *Nation* interview released in 2012, Lee Atwater, the architect behind the Willie Horton ads released during the 1988 Bush campaign, gives an even more glaring use of racism without race specificity. He reveals the spirit of the doctrine of the Southern strategy.

> You start out in 1954 by saying, Nigger, nigger, nigger. By 1968 you can't say nigger—that hurts you, backfires. So you say stuff like, uh, forced busing, states' rights, and all that stuff, and you're getting so abstract. Now, you're talking about cutting taxes, and all these things you're talking about are totally economic things and a byproduct of them is, blacks get hurt worse than whites and subconsciously maybe that is part of it. I'm not saying that. But, I'm saying that if it is getting that abstract and that coded, uh, that we're doing away with the racial problem one way or another, you follow me, cause obviously saying we want to cut this is much more abstract than even the busing thing, uh, and a hell of a lot more abstract than nigger, nigger, you know? So, any way you look at it, race is coming in on the back burner.[9]

The terms *urban* and *suburban* enjoyed a trajectory from clear geographic indicators to racial ones. During the 2020 presidential election cycle, President Trump vowed to protect the "suburban lifestyle dream" from low-income housing. The notion of government-subsidized housing invokes images of Black crime in the American social imagination. Stoking White fears that normalized White flight from our nation's cities to its suburbs, the president talked about race (and class) without talking about race. His administration rolled back an Obama-era provision that strengthened the Fair Housing Act's capacity to break up residential segregation by ensuring affordable housing in more affluent communities.

Trump tweeted, "Your housing prices will go up based on the market, and crime will go down."[10] Despite no evidence that crime was on the rise in majority-White suburbs, Trump marketed the overturn of the 2015 policy as a move to save neighborhoods and the American dream. His white noise said that Black bodies threaten the suburban utopia. Again, the leader of the free world talked about race without talking about race.

Sometimes what we call American and un-American is talking about race without talking about race. There is a local watering hole near my home that I enjoy frequenting. On multiple occasions, a Republican leader of a majority-White, affluent city has also been present. Our conversations often swell into outright disagreements about politics and religion, two conversational taboos between ideological rivals. Our clearest dividing line is in conversations about Trump. Nonetheless, that middle-aged White male Republican and this millennial Black pastor-activist continue to find ourselves in a collegial relationship.

One evening in 2017, I sauntered through the doors of the establishment. I was greeted by the leader's voice exclaiming that I needed to keep my boy Kaepernick off "their" football fields. He labeled the Black quarterback as an anti-American who was ruining the game. The polarizing athlete started his peaceful demonstration during "The Star-Spangled Banner" as a response to the unaccountability related to police-instigated killings of unarmed Black men, women, and children. My GOP associate accused Kaepernick of demeaning American values with his protest, maligning him as un-American for dramatizing how some Americans live unprotected.

It's not lost on me that when I saw this man in our usual place in mid-January of 2021, he made no mention of the January 6 insurrection. I had to initiate the conversation: "And you called Kaepernick un-American?"

"I don't want to talk about it, Willie," he said. Where was the outrage over White Americans storming the US Capitol and threatening to assassinate members of Congress? White ideology would not allow him to confess the staggering hypocrisy. It reserves "anti-American" for a Black activist-athlete, not White insurrectionists violently disrupting democratic proceedings.

The ubiquity of talking about race without talking about race begs that we confront these coded terms and substitutions for race when we hear them and utilize them. We should ask what we are trying not to say and why. Only by slowing the rhetoric down can we uncover the meaning and reveal who the language harms and who it benefits.

Too Heavy a Burden to Lift

Implicit racial bias saddles non-White people with undue burdens. If you have ever been the only one or one of the few persons of your racial identity, social class, or gender in a specific context, you at least vaguely know the pressure of maintaining composure and striving for perfection. The burden of representation converts our individual habits and performances into community perceptions and stereotypes. In work and school settings, the prevailing white noise disallows employees, students, and leaders of non-White communities to just be individuals. We unwillingly represent our entire identity group, knowing that opportunities for others depend on our performance. This burden forces us to talk, work, and engage in ways that disprove negative stereotypes. Individuality sinks in the seas of stereotypes when you live as a member of a marginalized people.

I took a class designed to probe the nature and mission of the global church—an unhelpful abstraction that I find often contributes to the silencing of non-White experiences and convictions. One week the professor assigned Dr. Raphael Warnock's *The Divided Mind of the Black Church*, one of the few texts in the course that raised the specter of race in American churches. The professor instructed all the Black students to explain what Warnock meant in his book. One by one, he called on us to speak for Warnock instead of offering our individual reflections. By contrast, the professor never asked White students to speak for John Wesley or Karl Barth. He consciously or unconsciously placed a burden on us to represent Black Christians and their traditions. We became Black interpreters of a Black experience for White people, even though one student had never attended a Black church and others departed from some of the book's foundational assumptions.

The burden of representation also impacts the ways non-White people interact with other non-White people. Many Black people live with curious cases of imposter syndrome and "survivor's remorse." White noise compels Black and Latinx folks to feel out of place despite wide-ranging experiences, irrefutable expertise, and earned credentials. This leaves us with a meandering sensation of regret, as if we failed to uphold accountability to old neighborhoods, classmates, and cousins. Even with the election of a Black man to the Oval Office, the election of a Black woman to the second-highest chair of democracy, and a growing Black millionaire class, the notion of Black success in the White corporate sphere continues to evade the assumptions of normativity.

Black women's career acceleration and upward mobility appear more normal in my circle of engagement than in most others, which is a signature of my class privilege. Nonetheless, a devout and imaginative lay leader of a church I served remarked about the abnormal prominence she wielded in the workplace despite the dual "demerits" linked to her gender and race. She described her excursion up the corporate ladder of a big tech company known the world over. She shared how she concealed her professional attainments in predominantly Black spaces. After forty years of intercessory prayer, corporate worship, and intentional relationships, she never shared a detail about her executive position to fellow church members because she didn't think Black people would believe she directed a department with so many secretaries and direct reports. Though this success brought pride, she kept it hushed so as not to create distance between her and others in the congregation. White noise contests the very notion of Black success, Black leadership, Black management, and Black supervisors.

Body Talk

A few weeks before the COVID-19 pandemic halted travel, I hosted a one-day training session in Tennessee. After sitting for two and a half hours, we walked across the hall of the school building into another classroom. I assembled multiple stations around the room, each representing a different broad social category (race/ethnicity, religion/faith, gender, sexuality/sex, citizenship, education, ability/disability, body image/size, and economic class).

I asked participants the following questions: "What identity are you most aware of?" "What identity do you rarely or never think about?" "Where do you experience the most privilege?" "Where do you experience the most social marginalization?" After each question, the group of nineteen scurried from station to station, exchanging stories and rationales. When I asked the group, "What identity do you believe people see first about you?" the thirteen non-White people all surrounded the race station, while the six White participants migrated to the stations for gender and sexuality. Together we discussed how they interpreted the fact that all the non-White people believed their race signaled public perceptions of them. What did that say about Whiteness?

One White participant responded, "This color is just a byproduct of human adaptability and response to climate. All skin is the same to me." One Black woman interjected, shrugging her shoulders, "I could get with that if my 'adaption to climate' did not license people to kill this Black body, impoverish this Black body, and fear this Black body." She underlined that our bodies carry stories of our experiences, ones invented by the doctrine of Whiteness. With little to no effort on our part, the body talks to us in the language of America. Racism, more specifically racial capitalism, is the native tongue of our land, saturated in the blood of indigenous Americans and Africans. Our bodies tell us how to act in certain settings and who belongs in certain spaces. Our bodies communicate stories about our employability and terminability, insurability and security, wealth and wellness, guilt and innocence.

Therefore, a syncopated identity accounts for the historical meanings of the body—the tropes, assumptions, and myths white noise whispers to us about phenotypical distinctions. Reparative intercession takes human bodies seriously. Bodily experience— the radicalized body particularly—is not incompatible with spirituality. Bodies ought to carry crucial significance for Christians, considering that a key symbol of this faith is the body of Jesus. Without frank honesty about Whiteness in the United States and US Christianity, White Christians live unbothered by the histories and terror their bodies encode on non-White bodies—bodies historically aligned with the marginalized, arrested, and executed body of Jesus.[11] This calls for a *kenōsis* (emptying) of our Christologies of their Whiteness.

History bears out that people form and practice theology out of their experiences—both social and personal. Despite assumptions of objectivity and eternal truth, our beliefs about God, Jesus, Scripture, and the like bespeak our race, gender, class, and other social identities. You may recall that my colorblind White seatmate on the flight abhorred such a position. The cultural influence on Christian beliefs and practice finds its greatest confirmation in the historical distinction between enslaved Africans on Christian plantations and the religious convictions of the enslavers and various enforcers of slavery.

An Americanized gospel, Christianity, and Jesus—all obliviously colorblind—create barriers for disrupting systemic racism. Jesus, historically and symbolically, could not be White given the histories of violence and the political-economic domination packed into the meaning of Whiteness. Likewise, the social context weathered by a first-century Palestinian Hebrew placed Jesus on the underside of said brutality and power.[12] Racial justice often halts at the altar of a White Christ—the popular image of Jesus that I distinguish from the Palestinian carpenter turned itinerant rabbi. For Christians, our Christologies impact our interpretations of Scripture and the witness of faith communities in the world. Highlighting Jesus's Hebrew identity confronts Americanized perversions of Christ used to embellish the foundations of White supremacy.

What is at stake for Whiteness and humanity, principally White Christians, if we dare to see Jesus as a victim of colonialism? The body of Christ—the global conglomeration of churches—must take seriously the body of Jesus, which was marginalized, poor, terrorized, arrested, and executed in a manger-to-cross pipeline. Followers of Jesus are students of a man born to a teenage mother, a once-infant refugee escaping the murderous insecurity of a puppet politician. Jesus was a religious leader profiled by the temple state: an incarcerated man facing trumped-up charges by a lynch mob who internalized Roman supremacy. He was denied a fair trial by a high court and executed by his government. Jesus was a man born into a lynched class that opposed the perception of the purity of their overlords in the Roman Empire.

Because of the oppositional definition of Blackness in the US, Black people live condemned to a chattel class, a lynched class, and an incarcerated class. Rome used a cross; America uses badges and bullets, electric chairs and electoral suppression, cells and sentences, deportation and detainment, ropes and rifles, cages and credit debt, and under-education and underemployment. If we are going to abolish systemic, implicit, and structural racism, the body of Christ must take seriously the body of Jesus as we save Black bodies. As Christians, we must honor the executed body of Jesus. Jesus's body matters to our spirituality and our struggle for racial repair. The Jesus of Palestine, untainted by the myths of American exceptionalism or the demands of capitalism, is an exemplar for breaking silence, realizing abolitionist spirituality, and combating racism and its economic incentives. The body of Jesus reminds us that our bodies carry horror stories long overdue for disruption and rewriting.

Storying the Self

White noise perpetuates stories about bodies, particularly bodies marked as substandard compared to the template of the White cisgender, heterosexual male body. Early in the process of fuller identity awareness, collective and individual habits portend the ease and comfort of living lost in stories of hierarchy. Reparative intercession subverts the preexisting racial narratives, narratives that fortify the fictive lines of heirarchical divides and validate the propensity to deny the deservedness of the most vulnerable. Syncopated identity asks for our hard-fought rejection of the stories that make sense because of the indelible ways society has impressed them on us. This way of *being* stories the self; it accounts for the implications of the multiple stories mapped onto our bodies reflective of our multiple intersecting identities.

History and place generate narratives we use to explain crime and success, family values and urban decay, and godliness and sinfulness in racial terms. When we cross to the other side of the street when Black youths approach or when we assume a person with Brown skin is an immigrant, we pull from knapsacks bursting at the seams with stereotyped stories. In our most intimate thoughts, we permit ourselves to harbor negative racial stereotypes without seeing ourselves as racist.

If we delay self-interrogation and recalibration, we will sleepwalk through life, prompted by white noise to remain unaccountable for our thoughts. We must dare to think introspectively about our implicit biases. Do we feel any burden, as human beings, to take responsibility for our private thoughts? Do our internal moral compass and faith challenge us to address what is undetectable by others? Reparative intercession and racial parrhesia (truth-telling) contribute to a public counternarrative about race—a story that commences with the self.

We stall the advent of racial justice and a higher version of the self when we flatten our lives to a single identity. The various social identities that contribute to our experiences in society should not be considered independent of one another. All of the identities we carry into the world speak to one another, thus impacting our social location. Intersectionality begs us to see the varied components of an individual as an amalgamation, a matrix of identifiers that mediate meaning for each other. Our gender informs the meaning of our race. Our race informs the meaning of our class. Our class—education, wealth, and occupation—informs our race. Syncopated identity makes us aware of how our many social selves relate to one another and the evolving world around us. We ought to concentrate on how our race speaks to our class, our race to our gender, and our race to our sexuality. We are most valuable to the cause of racial justice and abolition when we enter the work knowing we represent various social identities all in conversation with each other, pointing toward various points of privilege and underprivilege. Audre Lorde states, "There is no such thing as a single-issue struggle because we do not live single-issue lives."[13] The syncopated self defiantly explores the myriad issues that bump against its humanity and inherent dignity.

My identity as a Black man in the United States disinherits me from much of the promise of this nation. My experience bears the deep marks of racism, which invites police suspicion, impolite customer service, denial of due process, and assumptions of undeserved educational opportunities. But alongside the inequality posed by my race, I enjoy unearned privilege related to other facets of my identity. Ableism works to my advantage because I am not currently surviving physical, mental health, or cognitive disabilities. My Christianness protects me from the demonization experienced by Muslims and permits me to see my faith tradition reflected in my nation's symbolism. I live with citizenship privilege, heterosexual privilege, middle-class privilege, and, most certainly, male privilege. Even as people see a thing to fear when my Black body walks into certain spaces, I accrue social benefits because of many other aspects of my identity.

When I consider the racism I survive, I force myself to remember that Black women endure both racism and sexism, at a minimum, in various sectors of their lives. On the campus of a suburban California school, Joan, a Black grade-school teacher, often experiences tone policing, unwelcomed hands at the small of her back, and inquiries about natural hair. When I am reaching for my syncopated self, I picture myself outside a restaurant in Providence, Rhode Island, with one of my Morehouse brothers when I was first called a "nigger." Then I honor Samuel, a Latinx gay man who has been profiled as undocumented and was expelled from his church after he and his partner married.

It is also true that a poor White woman from rural Texas does not have the same scope of White privilege as an upper-middle-class White man from Austin. She knows racial privilege I will never know, but I possess a class privilege that reasons I have more in common with the middle-class White man than she does. Paradoxically, due to the nature of intersectional oppression, she and I likely have more in common experientially than either one of us has with him.

Syncopated identity is a counter-storytelling self, divesting from the untruth of justice-neutral stories. Toni Morrison opines, "Make up a story. Narrative is radical, creating us at the very moment it is being created."[14] To embrace the whole person, the intersectional self purges ideas and ways of thinking that compromise a social imagination inspired by multiracial mutuality, belonging, and agency. We need to tell ourselves new stories, stories unstained by White racism. Reparative narratives expand our capacity to see people as unique individuals undeserving of fears, insults, invalidations, and assaults.

What stories might contribute to a universal vocation of racial repair? What types of stories might aid our agency in the creation of a world of equality and sustainability? What types of stories do we need in order to see people as inherently worthy of protections and justice? How can we start to unlearn these stories?

Until the universality of the *imago Dei* dominates our racial thinking, we must create occasions to tell ourselves what we do not or no longer want to know. Karl Barth says, "If the Yes does not in some way contain the No, it will not be the Yes of a confession. . . . If we have not the confidence . . . to say *damnamus* [what we refuse], then we might as well omit the *credimus* [what we believe]."[15] Theologian Christopher Morse, whose work I first encountered while teaching theology at Sing Sing Correctional Facility in Ossining, New York, frames this as faithful disbelief—ideas we reject as Spirit people.[16] We purport to believe in equality, justice, oneness, and freedom, but our daily actions and inactions betray these values. If our beliefs have any validity, there are certain ideas we cannot espouse, privately or publicly. The only way to upend the stories that divide is to craft a new tale and put it on repeat. In practice, one tactic could be to make a list of the racial stories, myths, and stereotypes we reject and hang them somewhere accessible to us daily.

We should also develop a few reparative refutations. For example, because I believe in reparative racial justice, I refuse (1) any hierarchy of human lives, bodies, and cultures, (2) an image of God that makes any human being inferior or subjugated to any other human being, (3) the idea that racism is invulnerable to creative disruptions of human love, solidarity, and resilience, (4) to accept that racial repair and progress "roll in on the wheels of inevitability,"[17] and (5) any notions that socially determined race traits are biologically true. We should also formulate more particular examples of reparative refutations. I refuse to (1) fear Black and Brown bodies, (2) see otherness as defective, (3) allow discrimination to go unaddressed, (4) use Scripture to control people and legitimize bigotry, and (5) remain in racial silos.

Furthermore, increased cross-racial contact strips us of our ignorance and gives us a passport into the worlds and worldviews of others. This carries particular import for White people, many of whom live detached from non-White people save for what the media chooses to spotlight. We undo stories that feed our prejudice by doing life with othered persons. Racial avoidance, both experiential and conversational, underwrites our discomfort and stereotypes that are constructed and consumed from a distance. Cross-racial contact opens our eyes to see Black and Brown people as real persons who are loving, creating, thinking, and loved individuals, not just anonymous members of a group defined by the schema and logic of race. We form an awareness of our syncopated selves—our full, layered, intersectional selves—through deliberate contact with the other.

Intersectional thinking and interracial exploration reveal the matrix of domination upsetting our peace. They urge us to deposit counter-stories into our memory banks. We show up in public radically self-aware, which creates the opportunity for the Spirit to shake us free of our insistence that there is a racial hierarchy. We can live according to new stories, memorized to release us from the sin of Whiteness that ranks human bodies, reinforces powerlessness through division, and nurtures our fears of dark skin.

Moreover, to find this reparative self, we undertake the consuming task of tracing our lives backward to move forward. The Spirit propositions us to go back in our memories, and when we reach our earliest conscious memory of our self, we can take a quantum leap and find the great I Am—the common denominator of all flesh. Trace yourself back to your earliest embodied memory, one of the first times you were cognizant of your racial identity, and then remember there was a *you* and a *them* before that. We lived in the presence of the eternal God as worthy and deserving before we drew our first breaths. We were beautifully endowed with our phenotypic particularities in the mind of God before we entered time through the passageway of a woman's womb—the canal of the sacred. We own our humanity on the basis that God is the parent of every living category of the universe. Any other framing of human flesh ranks partial at best, and destructive in so many cases.

"It's not my job to fix racism."

5

Pulse to Risk

Sacrificing Our Power and Privilege

A few winters ago, a local high school booster club invited me to offer the keynote address at a celebration for their football team after an emotionally charged semester and sports season. With unparalleled athleticism, the young men managed to make history as a ball club and attract the attention of the state during playoffs. But only a couple months prior, the football stadium had morphed into a firing range, inflicting wounds that will not soon heal. In a mass shooting, a ten-year-old boy of promise and effervescence lost his life to gun violence. His murder froze the hopes and comforts of the county and halted a stellar football season. Many members in our congregation knew the boy as a relative or knew his mother and grandmother as friends of their family.

I arrived at the country club for the annual celebration of players and parents keenly aware of the tension with which these Black and Brown boys lived. I hoped to celebrate their victories and attend to their pain. So many of them lived under the unchecked threat of gun violence—in addition to the daily trials of food scarcity and opportunity apartheid. Undoubtedly, this was a high moment of pride and possibility. During my twenty-minute speech, I took less than a minute to say, "You are the embodied hope our communities need. This hope outlives last night's growl of a stomach due to a missed meal or tomorrow's endurance of a teacher's inability to understand the unrelenting pressures of living Black or Latinx in America." I sat down confident that the young men heard me commiserate with their experiences.

After I returned to the head table, a few people affirmed the speech as appropriate for the occasion and audience. However, as I reached to dress my salad, a White chemistry teacher glared at me. "Please pass me the salad dressing," I said to provide an opening for him to express himself.

"Are you sure you're a pastor?" he inquired. "I'm offended you told these boys White teachers don't understand them. Talking about race only makes race an issue."

"If we avoid talking about race," I responded, "we actually deny these young men's experiences and allow racism to fester."

He rebutted my claim by suggesting my invocation of racism was the only racism these boys experienced within the school system. After several moments of debate, he added his opinion that talking about racism cannot end racism. For him, only God can end racism. He myopically assumed my career as a pastor signaled I shared his understanding of racism as just another sin, a spiritual condition. Jesus died because sin will never go away; therefore, racism will never go away. The teacher assumed that as long as there is sin and a devil, there will be racism. With such flagrant pessimism and resignation, it is no wonder he held that people only make our racial situation worse by talking about it.

White noise tells us that racism is not solvable and that talking about it, even in the forms of reparative intercession or racial parrhesia (truth-telling), only entrenches us in racial pessimism. Our imaginations, so infected by our persistent existing conditions, cancel even the possibility of any vague semblance of hope that racism has a death date. White noise lures us into a defeatism that easily accepts the everlasting character of Whiteness. It cancels our capacity to see beyond the headlines of another George Floyd or the rote dynamics of our uniracial residential bubbles and dream wholeheartedly in ways that transgress the status quo.

Racial pessimism amounts to a spiritual crisis. For scores of people of faith, this attitude feeds the view that racism is an inextricable feature of the human condition—sinful and fallen. Said resignation grows out of an understanding of sin as inherent to all humanity and beyond human correction. It implies that only God can end racism or that racism is an unending consequence of the "fall from grace." These hardened doctrines distort the God-originating nature of humanity and blame the crises of racism on God. We let ourselves rinse our hands of remedying racism and find a hiding place behind this god of absolution and apathy. We use this god to duck the demands of the God of love, who invites us into a new identity and imagination meant to overturn the destructive forces of Whiteness.

James Baldwin's insight proves beneficial here. The Harlem-born literary artist criticized American Christianity for masking self-hatred and perverse self-absolution. In his typical manner, Baldwin determined, "Jesus . . . knew all the secrets of my heart. Perhaps He did, but I didn't, and the bargain we struck, actually down there at the foot of the cross, was that He would never let me find out. He failed his bargain. He was a much better Man than I took Him for."[1] Here Baldwin raises the specter of an unspoken bargain made with God that clears us of the responsibility for bringing into being a beloved, re-created world that honors the image of a loving God of freedom in all flesh. This is white noise telling us it's God's work; it's not my fault; it's not my responsibility. As we cower behind the small print of the bargain, absolving ourselves of this responsibility to work toward justice, some Black students receive lesson plans two grades under their level, groups of Latinx children live hunted by ICE, Trumpism dominates state and federal politics, and the racial wealth gap sucks families into a quicksand of nihilism. These are the social implications of spiritual bypassing.

In the 1980s, prominent psychotherapist John Welwood described spiritual bypassing as the "tendency to use *spiritual* ideas and practices to sidestep or avoid facing unresolved emotional issues, psychological wounds, and unfinished developmental tasks."[2] For our purposes, spiritual bypassing means ignoring our society's race questions by using religious practices and ideas. We use religious doctrine to understand racial inequities as something natural to the cosmic order and thus use this to excuse our inaction. Believing that racism is inevitable frees us from doing the work of anti-racism, even while we believe that physical diseases and hunger can and should be eliminated.

When white noise drowns out the hope for social transformation and our capacity to achieve it, we must practice a fifth rhythm of reparative intercession, the pulse to risk—risking power and privilege to broaden our sacred imagination so we can construct a new social order anchored in human dignity, equality, and sustainability. Anna Julia Cooper, American educator and sociologist, posits, "The cause of freedom is not the cause of a race or a sect, a party or a class—it is the cause of human kind, the very birthright of humanity."[3] We guard freedom as a human birthright through risks. The pulse to risk lowers the high frequency of ideas that reduce us to racial resignation and pessimism, damning us to tragic inaction and privileged distance.

Racial justice requires a redistribution of power. Among themselves and in public, White people must dare to discuss what they are willing to sacrifice—what power and privilege they are willing to give up—in service of sustaining the stated promise of America and living into its founding creeds. Black men must consider what we must give up to advance justice for Black women and the Black queer community. Racial justice, equally, asks Black middle-class communities to risk their class privilege for poor Black folks. The same holds true for Latinx communities and their various intersecting shades of social life. Risking power and privilege is holy because it puts us in touch with a fuller meaning of humanity. Risk is the heartbeat of faith. Without risk, faith fails before we arrive at moments that call us to courageously pursue the abolition of racism in the self and on interpersonal and structural levels.

Though consistently painful, we must take our power and privilege to the altar of justice and sacrifice them daily. A number of the social privileges we should be willing to sacrifice and risk for racial repair and justice come to mind:

- a racialized system of legacy college admissions;
- the faux protections of our inaction on racial discrimination and injustices;
- the pretensions of colorblindness;
- the penchant to advance opportunities only for other White people;
- a willful ignorance about the way race functions to open or close opportunities;
- the belief that Jesus of Nazareth was White;
- "safe" distance from the violence that threatens poor Black and Brown lives;
- a delusion that our religious convictions do not harm others;
- the myth that all American heroes are White;
- the normalization of White superiority in grade school curricula;
- convictions that crime is Black;
- a sense of entitlement to jobs and capital development opportunities;

- and the unquestioned freedom to live in segregated communities of safety, influence, and affluence.

The immolation of the lines that divide and define our lives and bodies sparks a spirituality we can feel from our bones to our skin.

A pulse to risk positions us to withdraw from counterproductive affiliations, be intentional about cross-racial contact, and refuse to support entities with self-avowed predilections for discrimination or a documented reputation of privileging White people. This requires researching said entities before we spend, invest, contract, attend, and enroll. What a difference it makes to draw attention to the crises—injustices, discrimination, and disparities—besieging our communities.

Another Look at Jesus: Abolitionist Spirituality

Jesus the carpenter embodied the pulse to risk. Put at the center of our lives, justice and freedom charge us to conduct an examination of our faith commitments—a routine experience of listening, feeling, and inspecting various parts of our faith communities and personal beliefs. The late Peter Gomes, in *The Scandalous Gospel of Jesus*, penned, "The question should not be 'What would Jesus do?' but rather, more dangerously, 'What would Jesus have me do?' The onus is not on Jesus but on us, for Jesus did not come to ask semi-divine human beings to do impossible things. He came to ask human beings to live up to their full humanity; he wants us to live in the full implication of our human gifts, and that is far more demanding."[4] Life in the Jesus movement is a sacred solicitation to find our place in the work of abolition—to come alive at the faintest recognition of our profuse power to love the ones not like us.

Jesus's manifesto in Luke 4:18–19 confirms the spirituality of justice, the sacredness of the political done humanely. Per the custom, the chief ruler of the synagogue requests that someone from the congregation read a passage from Isaiah. On this particular

Sabbath, the worship leader identifies Jesus to read, assuming him to be one of the few literate persons in the stigmatized, ghettoized, and abandoned sections of Galilee. There are not yet chapter and verse divisions. So, after the leader hands Jesus the scroll, Jesus unrolls the parchment and fingers his way to Isaiah 61. After the recitation of the Shema and the eighteen benedictions, Jesus stands to read a slightly customized version of the first two verses of this prophetic text: "The Spirit of the Lord is upon me, because he has anointed me to bring good news to the poor. He has sent me to proclaim release to the captives and recovery of sight to the blind, to let the oppressed go free, to proclaim the year of the Lord's favor" (Luke 4:18–19)—which happens to be one of my favorite passages of biblical text.

Jesus's reading of the Hebrew text departs from the original Isaiah text in some ways. The writers or editors of Luke depict Jesus omitting the phrases "to bind up the brokenhearted" and "the day of vengeance of our God." Further, he incorporates a phrase from Isaiah 58:6: "let the oppressed go free." Nonetheless, of all the many excoriating jewels in Isaiah, Jesus lands here. He uses this passage as the basis for his first sermon. The carpenter foregrounds an agenda designed to impact the lives of the unprotected. Good news to the poor is anti-poverty economic policies. Setting the captive free is criminal justice reform. Recovery of sight to the blind is guaranteeing affordable healthcare. Setting the oppressed free is emancipation. Proclaiming the year of the Lord's favor is reparation.

It took me years to see how radical this rhetorical moment in the ministry of Jesus was—much more radical than appears to the naked eye. Leviticus 25 stipulates that the Hebrews observe the Jubilee every fiftieth year, which included freeing slaves and canceling debt. The year of the Lord's favor, described in Leviticus 25:10, was a year of wealth, redistribution, land redemption, and reparations. What is radical to us today appeared to pop off the scroll and flow off Jesus's tongue as a normal religious-political mainstay.

The witness of the carpenter—steeped in his own formation as a Hebrew devotee to the God of the exodus—compels us to act on behalf of and in solidarity with disinherited, marginalized people. The responsibility to combat systemic injustices inheres the life of faith, dispatching all constituents of Spirit people to deploy their gifts and disciplines in service of human liberation, vis-à-vis racial justice. Even the imperative of the exodus in the Judeo-Christian traditions pulls us toward abolitionist spirituality. The Hebrew faith—the religion *of* Jesus, not the religion *about* Jesus—organizes around and originates from the mass migration of enslaved people out of the Egyptian empire. This moment is unambiguously political. The cultural and spiritual memory that animates Hebrew life relates to the exodus—human liberation through a political innovation rooted in a divine disruption. A new exodus from Whiteness, patriarchy, queer phobias, and poverty—to enumerate only a few origins of crisis—rewinds our memory to lay claim to the wisdom of yesterday.

The political without the spiritual is predatory and loveless. The spiritual without the political is passive and unproductive. Abolitionist spirituality reflects a political spirituality come alive through behaviors that feed countercultural truths and unselfish interactions with those perceived as disposable. Michel Foucault gives this definition, "political spirituality is . . . a set of practices undertaken to loosen the power of regimes of truth that tell us who we are and to critique those regimes . . . and thus to loosen the power of the identities that have been imposed on us, that are us."[5] This work is personal but never private. It welcomes the other into future-sharing, life-affirming, public-improving transformation. Changing the consciousness of individuals only matters if we transform the institutional and structural production of truth. Justice is where the political and the spiritual rendezvous.

Therefore, abolitionist spirituality is the critical and imaginative embodiment of visions of the God of liberation, for this world that treats the human person as holy and deserving of love and freedom vis-à-vis changing systems of disinheritance and structural sin. A person with the pulse to risk for abolition sees the end of oppression and gives fully of themselves without permitting the daily pain to reify the norms. This socially conscious, freedom-anchoring spirituality critiques the status quo, centers the lived experiences of unprotected peoples, and casts a glimpse of this world with new social and relational arrangements. Roughly, I identify five invitations of abolitionist spirituality that guide the pulse to risk: (1) a daily preferential option for the unprotected, (2) a sacred intolerance of the iniquity of inequities, (3) urgent, active disruptions of hegemonic structures, (4) reparation for harm to the bodies and minds of the violated, and (5) a daily renewal of a counter-imagination and reconstructive action. As an act of holiness, we must transform the very material and logical conditions that perpetuate and protect injustice. In this sense, reparative intercessors live out an abolitionist spirituality. Each invitation inheres risks that contribute to the practice of freedom apropos to transform the person and the public. Abolitionist spirituality clears the way within us to perform more magnanimous risk-responsive interventions in the world.

A Daily Preferential Option for the Unprotected

A daily preferential option for the unprotected costs us time, comfort, resources, and relationships as we leave the safety of non-participation in service of people who are left behind. In his initial sermon, as reflected in Luke's gospel, Jesus frames the spiritual life as a quest to discover what it really means to be human, a way of becoming that is inaccessible to the brutalities of selfishness. "The Spirit of the Sovereign LORD is on me, because the LORD has anointed me to proclaim good news to the poor" (Isa. 61:1 NIV). A number of Hebrew Bible scholars argue that these words, placed at the center of the final section of Isaiah (56–66), come from the period just after the end of the Babylonian exile. Jesus's declaration of a justice-centered vocation is a message both to exiles and those left behind—captives preparing to migrate home on a reconstruction mission and the Israelities left to live among the religious, economic, and political ruins of their homeland for roughly seven decades.

In fact, the words of the ancient text epitomize a lively tenet of abolitionist spirituality: "The spirit of the Lord GOD is upon me, because the LORD has anointed me; he has sent me to bring good news to the poor." The word translated "poor" in the New International Version is the Hebrew word 'anawim. This category of peoples in post-exilic Israel likely represented the large segment of Hebrews exploited by the ruling, law-literate, land-grabbing class. The ancient Israelite world labeled them *ammi ha-aretz*—people of the land. They were the means of production commodified to serve the interests of the local and international elite.

Am ha-aretz (the singular of *ammi ha-aretz*) connoted an "ignorant" or "boorish" person in this ancient culture. To the rabbinic guilds of the Talmud, an *am ha-aretz*, by virtue of their ignorance, was deemed lax in their observance of the commandments. As a group, they were a despised, disposable, and derogated class of people in the ancient world. In post-exilic Israel, the disparaging term exclusively referred to persons left behind in the ruins after the Babylonian conquest of Judea, as well as their descendants. As people of the land and descendants of the left behind, they lived under the insanity of bigotry and the racialized classist stereotypes of their own people.

Originally, this label simply meant people who were agricultural workers. According to Dr. Obery Hendricks, "However, by the end of the Exile in 539 B.C., *am ha-aretz* had begun to have a distinctly negative connotation, as in Nehemiah 10:30, in which the returned exiles declared about those who had remained behind and apparently intermarried with Gentiles, 'We will not give our daughters to the *am-ha-aretz* (people of the land) or take their daughters for our sons.' By the first century the term had become fully negative, designating all Jews who did not abide by the prescriptions of the Law."[6] The derisive tenor of the label cast persons as the lowest specimen with the lowest character. Priests regularly demeaned the people of the land. Hendricks describes one such hyperbole: "A man . . . should not marry the daughter of an *am ha-aretz*, because they are detestable and their wives vermin, and of their daughters it is said, 'Cursed be he who lies with any kind of beast.' . . . In this sense, *am ha-aretz* might best be understood as the Hebrew equivalent of 'nigger.'"[7] These were basically sharecropping, landless workers subject to a tiny ruling class and landlords.

Abolitionist spirituality requires risk-responsive solidarity with the oppressed, the left behind, the abandoned, the dehumanized, the rejected, and those whom Ida B. Wells-Barnett might call "the sinned against."[8] A practical realization of persistent neighborliness is solidarity. When we practice solidarity, we risk questioning authorities about marginalization and turn opportunities aside in order to benefit historically underprivileged persons. Radical unity with the unprotected asks us to opt out of inclusion when the othered are excluded or underrepresented and to disassociate from certain networks and persons when our alliances threaten the dignity of the othered. Those practicing solidarity calculate the risks and lean in.

The oppressed of our time remain those who are looted of their land and labor, history and honor by the theatrics and terror of chattel slavery. Every day presents a choice to live in solidarity with the unprotected, with those victimized by Whiteness, which is idolatrous, demonic, and segregationist. Every day presents a choice to pledge allegiance to abolition for the left behind through radical, sustainable practices and structures that serve human fulfillment and justice, unlike the fragile freedoms experienced since the end of the Civil War. Our spirituality evolves our humanity when we risk for the unprotected among us.

Heralded as the Moses of America, Harriett Tubman—a courageous, God-centered freedom fighter—braved the volatility of the antebellum South in her campaign for Black freedom. She risked capture and death during every reparative intercessory rescue mission, and her success mocked the intelligence and firepower of her detractors. As a twelve-year-old, Tubman entered a local dry-goods store to obtain supplies for her captors. While at the store, she witnessed another enslaved person, who had left the fields without permission, experience the intense violence normative to the slave condition. His overseer demanded that Tubman help restrain him. Instead, Tubman used her body as a barricade in the doorway, where she stood in the tragic gap to allow the enslaved person to escape. The White man threw a weight at the runaway man, but it landed on her head. It is suggested she may have suffered from temporal lobe epilepsy as a result of the injury.

The trauma of the injury caused seizures that rendered her unconscious, although she maintained that she was aware of her surroundings. Nonetheless, people were unable to wake her when she suddenly lost consciousness, which she framed as visions. With nineteen successful freedom missions from the North into the slaveholding states, she called her visions, which led her through swamps and woods, trails and rivers, "consulting with God."[9] Every risk for the enslaved, the unprotected, was a communication with God—a form of prayer. Reportedly, she once fell asleep beneath a wanted poster displaying her photo, a multi-thousand-dollar reward, and the words "Wanted Dead or Alive."

Tubman knew that if a passenger changed their mind about pursuing freedom in the North or Canada, the entire freedom project would be jeopardized. So, when a passenger expressed second thoughts, Tubman pulled out a gun and said to the group, "You'll be free or die a slave!"[10] Tubman's assertive posture and hope-abundant rhetoric were more persuasive than her gun. Though Tubman risked her life as a conductor of this clandestine network of safe houses and wooded trails, she refused to jeopardize the sacredness of her freedom mission and the lives entrusted to her. She enfleshed a steady and radical leave-no-one-behind article of faith.

Tubman lived consumed by risk-responsive solidarity—a history and message pulsating at the center of abolitionist spirituality.[11]

Those who follow a daily preferential option for the unprotected elect to journey with them. By choosing to center the needs, vision, and experiences of the unprotected, these people exhibit the pulse to risk, which causes them to ask the following:

- Who are the left behind among us?
- What historical factors locked them out?
- Why did/didn't this happen to me and my racial group?
- How do/would I live in their condition(s)?

A Sacred Intolerance of the Iniquity of Inequities

The pulse to risk freely gives up racial pessimism. Abolitionist spirituality invites us to nurture a sacred intolerance of racism—along with all other forms of oppression. Hendricks describes this as "treating the needs of people as holy."[12] Reparative intercessors and abolitionists frame social problems as moral and theological issues. During the antebellum period, abolitionists excoriated slavery as a sin—a systemic sin and an institutional iniquity. These opponents of enslavement maintained that "sin could not be solved by political compromise or sociological reform."[13] The answer to systemic sin is a new social order grounded in human sustainability, dignity, and equality.

Jesus deliberately said, "The Spirit of the Lord is upon me." The Spirit resources and initiates this work. *Ruah* in Hebrew and *pneuma* in Greek, this divine wind carries the courageously openhearted beyond the insularities of fear and the selfish enclaves of indifference. God blows oxygen into the work of justice when we dare to leverage our power and privilege for those not like us. Abolitionist spirituality transcends the cannibalizing partisan drama of blue donkeys and red elephants. It mobilizes humans to contribute to the reimagination and re-creation of society. The Spirit produces more than an ecstatic encounter with God; the Spirit births a heightened sense of calling based on love that nurtures a desire to help those not like us.

The work of the Spirit must center the liberation of oppressed communities. Public resistance to structures of domination requires embracing the prophethood of all believers. The late Harvard Divinity School professor James Luther Adams placed the priesthood of all believers alongside the prophethood of all believers. He wrote that a prophetic church "is a church in which all members share in the common responsibility to attempt to foresee the consequences of human behavior (both individual and institutional) with the intention of making history in place of merely being pushed around by it. Only through the prophetism of all believers can we together foresee doom and mend our common ways."[14] The democracy of the Spirit—our universal accessibility to and equality in the God of freedom—breathes life into our public love. Anyone can do this work with the right risk-responsive posture.

As Spirit people—people who throw themselves into the love revolution unencumbered by the trappings of colorblind Christianity—we practice a pneumatic politic of love. In her essay "Love as the Practice of Freedom," bell hooks writes, "The moment we choose to love we begin to move against domination, against oppression. The moment we choose to love we begin to move towards freedom, to act in ways that liberate ourselves and others. That action is the testimony of love as the practice of freedom."[15] A person never achieves reparative intercession or an abolitionist devotion without an embodied disdain for oppression. Only a mass exhibition of abundant humanity—the practice of radical mutuality, love beyond the limits of our prejudices, prudent local power analyses, and authentic vulnerability—can furnish the resources necessary to combat the social nihilism, political defeatism, and moral panic besieging our lives.

The antebellum period houses examples of the deep alignment between spirituality and abolition. Abolition clears the passageways of our souls so we can sing with the people and for the people. William Lloyd Garrison penned a hymn, sung to the tune of "Auld Lang Syne," to fire up the abolitionist cause in 1841.

> I am an Abolitionist!
> Oppression's deadly foe;
> In God's great strength will I resist,
> And lay the monster low;
> In God's great name do I demand,
> To all be freedom given,
> That peace and joy may fill the land,
> And songs go up to heaven!
>
> I am an Abolitionist!
> No threats shall awe my soul,
> No perils cause me to desist,
> No bribes my nets control;
> A freeman will I live and die,
> In Sunshine and in shade,
> And raise my voice for liberty,
> Of nought on earth afraid.[16]

Being "spiritual" does not mean escaping the world but rather a creative engagement with the poor and beleaguered of the world. God pulls us into each morning as enfleshed revelations poised to strip bare the pretensions of White male supremacist sin camouflaged in the fabric of our politics and religion and ready to take part in abolitionist action.

When we have the pulse to risk, a manifestation of sacred intolerance, we ask:

- What renews my will to speak up and show up?
- Who do I trust to hold me accountable?

145

- What aspects of my faith community impede an ongoing commitment to racial truth-telling and racial justice?
- What aspects of my faith feed an ongoing commitment to racial truth-telling and racial justice?
- What might it mean to pray with my legs?

Urgent, Active Disruptions of Hegemonic Structures

When we shake ourselves free from gradualism, our lives begin to subvert the justice delayed and denied, which holds anti-racism hostage. Abolitionist spirituality invites us to immediate and ongoing collective practices designed to disrupt structural sins and iniquitous systems. Racial justice requires solidarity with and self-sacrifice for the other; true racial justice cannot hide behind inert sensations of sympathy or isolated acts of charity. The quiet sympathies of good people will not initiate the emergence of a true public good for all. Sympathy—disembodied, non-proximal feelings of concern—is a costless response to racial injustice. James Cone clarifies: "Christian Communities join the cause of the oppressed in the fight for justice not because of some philosophical principle of 'the Good' or because of a religious feeling of sympathy for people in prison. Sympathy does not change the structures of injustice. The authentic identity of Christians with the poor is found in the claim which the Jesus-encounter lays upon their own life-style, a claim that connects the word 'Christian' with the liberation of the poor."[17] Sometimes sympathy unwittingly cooperates with injustice when feelings of despondency, gloom, shock, and indignation never rise above silence. Feelings without action are dead and often leave a significant body count of dead and dying Black and Latinx people in their trail. Justice, racial or otherwise, is a doing. At best, sympathy is a front door to our reasonable service of reparative disruptions.

In *Ferguson and Faith: Sparking Leadership and Awakening Community*, Leah Gunning Francis writes, "To do justice for the oppressed is to correct the injustice that is being done, not to only provide a balm for the hurts that have been caused."[18] Charity addresses immediate needs created by systemic inequalities. Justice addresses the root causes of systemic inequalities. I define social justice as the guarantee of human equality, sustainability, and dignity through the redistribution of material resources and the dismantling of oppressive structures.

The following parable, relayed by my mentor, J. Alfred Smith Sr., offers vivid imagery for grasping and decoding the two forms of public engagement.

A villager sees a baby floating down the river. He jumps in the water and saves the baby, but the next day he finds two more babies floating down the river. Again, he saves the babies, but on the following day he sees four babies. The number keeps growing each day, and soon the entire village is diligently working to save more and more babies. Quickly overwhelmed by the task, a woman among the villagers eventually raises the question of where all the babies are coming from. It is proposed that a team be organized to go up the river to the source of the problem.[19]

The woman in the parable realizes the community is addressing the symptoms of the problem by pulling the babies out of the water. Each day, as the number of drowning babies multiplies, the members of the village roll up their sleeves, hike up their bottoms, and fish vulnerable life out of the troubling waters. Community service, as necessary as it is, is downstream work that treats the symptoms of massive problems like racism and poverty. Social justice—a more expansive category—requires going upstream to cut off the sources of the problems.

Downstream interventions offer opportunities for daily, individual survival, while upstream disruptions strive for the end of the death-making systems themselves. There is no question that racially stigmatized, strategically impoverished, and neglected communities require both downstream and upstream engagement; however, we must know the difference when considering the impact we hope to realize.

Related to hunger, downstream work involves soup kitchens and food pantries, while upstream approaches necessitate campaigning for higher minimum wages and job accessibility. Downstream activity supports the efforts of tutorial programs and career days, while upstream initiatives look like marching for equity in education funding and culturally responsive curricula. When considering the pervasive crisis of racialized policing, downstream projects involve coordinating community-police basketball tournaments for youth, while upstream interruptions involve petitioning to defund militarized police equipment and mandating anti-racism training for law enforcement personnel. To address mass incarceration, downstream work necessitates visits to prisons for the purposes of worship and Bible study, while upstream ministry involves advocating for economic policies that protect the most vulnerable or lobbying on behalf of nonviolent offenders.

The Brazilian archbishop Dom Helder Camara testified, "When I feed the poor, they call me a saint, but when I ask why the poor are hungry, they call me a communist."[20] The "why" ruffles feathers, polarizes the issue, clarifies the parties to blame, and looks for remedies to the problem in question. Justice works to end the circumstances of inequality that make charity necessary.

Justice requires a risk of power and privilege. Some disruptive practices that draw inspiration from abolitionist spirituality include joining nonviolent direct action, advocating for policy changes, calling for curricula redevelopment in schools, examining our spheres of influence, educating decision-makers according to a liberative vision, and bringing our anti-racism to our decision-making roles.

To abolish White hegemony, we must embrace the pulse to risk and ask:

- What racial justice issue most disturbs me? Why?
- Who benefits from the existing arrangement?
- Who is most violated by the existing arrangement?
- What is a downstream approach to this issue?
- What is an upstream approach to this issue?
- Who is already doing something?

Reparation for Harm to the Bodies and Minds of the Violated

Abolitionist spirituality invites us to repair the material and psychic harms inflicted on unprotected racial communities. Five overlapping generations of African peoples lived under the American tyranny that snatched children from the arms of defenseless mothers and sold devoted fathers up the river without a moment's notice. In the center of town, slavery profiteers marched caravans of innocent flesh toward their most unimaginable nightmare, which started at the auction block and ended in an unmarked, shallow grave.

Abolitionist spirituality underscores the psychological violence of what I call plantation religion—the use of dogma, ritual, and doctrine to protect White power, still at work in certain brands of Christianity today. In the middle of dehumanizing Christian hate and exploitation, brush harbor spirituality cleared out sacred space for Black bodies to rediscover God unstained by the colossal perversions of the religion of Whiteness. Beyond the gaze of Whiteness, the brush harbor offered an enduring and clandestine feature for Black survival during plantation life, where unmediated experiences of the God of freedom could occur. My ancestors picked cotton and tobacco; cleaned houses and raised masters' children; slept in unprotected, unstable housing; were whipped from the auction block to the outhouse; ate scraps; and witnessed children sold and women raped. However, on Sunday, a quasi-off day, they made their way to the brush harbor—an invisible sanctuary in the woods—to worship in freedom. Our ancestors understood the value of just arriving in the sanctuary.

In Toni Morrison's *Beloved*, when Sethe, the protagonist, determines that "it was time to lay it all down," she heads to the woods to find the Clearing—the brush harbor. It is there, she recalls, that Baby Suggs, the unchurched preacher born into slavery, exhorted her community:

> Here, in this here place, we flesh; flesh that weeps, laughs; flesh that dances on bare feet in grass. Love it. Love it hard. Yonder they do not love your flesh. They despise it. . . . No more do they love the skin on your back. And O my people they do not love your hands. Those they only use, tie, bind, chop off and leave empty. Love your hands! Love them. Raise they up and kiss them. Touch others with them, pat them together, stroke them on your face 'cause they don't love that either. . . . You got to love it, you. This is flesh I'm talking about here. Flesh that needs to be loved. . . . And O my people, out yonder, hear me, they do not love your neck unnoosed and straight. So love your neck.[21]

This brush harbor preaching offered new stories for bodies and minds condemned by stories of the land. This sounded like good news to the victims of the American organized conspiracy of anti-Blackness. Baby Suggs's affirmation of Black flesh, beyond the gaze and authority of White power, models a vocabulary for a new way of knowing and being. The pulse to risk in the name of material and psychic repair negates normative messaging and storying of the violated.

The Spirit leaves a small, unsettling voice in the center of our being that points us toward creating safe and brave space for the sinned against. I see this living beneath the work of Jesus, through the Beatitudes and other parts of the Sermon on the Mount. Jesus calls the stigmatized, poor, exploited *ammi ha-aretz*—people of the land—blessed, the salt of the earth, and the light of the world. He creates a counternarrative for victims of the temple state. A counternarrative to Black inferiority must supplant the centuries-old messages so normalized by media, churches, and curricula. Oppressed people the world over deserve safe space—brush harbors in the middle of metropolises of inequality and dread. We heal psychic wounds when we publicly and privately share racial truths unstained by the ugly history we love to forget and invest in safe and brave spaces created and operated by unprotected peoples doing the work to re-story Black and Latinx lives and critique dominant perceptions of Whiteness.

To repair the harm inflicted on the bodies and minds of the violated, we must embrace the pulse to risk and ask:

- Where do I consume negative messages about Black and Latinx people?
- What are some stereotypes about Black and Latinx people? Which do I believe personally?
- What are ways to build a counternarrative to racial stereotypes I believe? (As explored in chap. 3.)
- What steps can I take to contribute to a public counternarrative to racial stereotypes?

A Daily Renewal of a Counter-imagination and Reconstructive Action

Reconstructive thinking and acting help us resolve to give up an attachment to the way things are. The work to eradicate racial injustice continues to exhibit a failure of imagination and moral will. I place emphasis here on our failure of imagination to see the world wholly reordered away from the rules that govern our national life. Emancipation, voting rights, attaining citizenship, and low-wage jobs have never sufficed to undo the destabilizing devastations of American slavery. For people of faith, abolition is a spirituality of reparative and re-creative action. America, as a multiracial democracy, is only possible when we structurally invest in forming a democracy that guarantees resource equity for the disinherited, dispossessed, and disenfranchised. This requires stirring our imaginations for what we have never seen.

After 246 years of forced labor and a soul-shattering relationship with Whiteness, mere freedom for the enslaved was never enough. In an uncelebrated remark, Martin Luther King Jr. professed, "America freed the slaves in 1863, . . . but gave the slaves no land, and nothing in reality. . . . It refused to give its black peasants from Africa, who came here involuntarily in chains and had worked free for two hundred and forty-four years, any kind of economic base. And so emancipation for the Negro was really freedom to hunger. It was freedom to the winds and rains of Heaven. It was freedom without food to eat or land to cultivate and therefore was freedom and famine at the same time."[22] Though the Baptist preacher from Georgia curiously dates emancipation in 1863, he is right in his acknowledgment that freedom alone failed to guarantee protection and justice for formerly enslaved Africans in America.

Abolition requires creative, constructive institutions and new economic arrangements. The abolitionist tradition seeks to broaden democracy and expand the political window of equity and human flourishing. Without a proactive posture toward human becoming, we fail to see big enough ways to give people what they need before they misuse or distort their humanity.

Abolitionist spirituality invites us to renew our imagination, language, and actions. American racism arrests our collective and personal imaginations, threatening Black and Latinx people with apathy and animosity. The chattel imagination normalizes the ways Black communities endure the unrelenting blows dealt by mass inequities in schools, corporate offices, health companies, and the legal system. So many people live trapped in place due to what Willie James Jennings calls "a diseased social imagination,"[23] which distorts our perceptions of race and disfigures the lived outcomes of non-White people. The chattel imagination is the mental schema that crowns Whiteness as the ideal and perceives Black people as inherently deserving of control, isolation, punishment, inhumanity, and exclusion. The gross familiarity of White privilege and power confiscates our will to see a world without them.

Percy Bysshe Shelley, in "A Defence of Poetry," offers, "A man, to be greatly good, must imagine intensely and comprehensively; he must put himself in the place of another and of many others; the pains and pleasures of his species must become his own. The great instrument of moral good is the imagination."[24] Imagination requires more complex neural activity because it cannot depend on the familiarity of memory and lived experiences. Eddie Glaude purports, "[Imagination] motivates us to act for what is possible and not settle for things as they are, and helps us see the fullness of the humanity of those with whom we live."[25] A mutual sacred imagination demands that we risk our power and privilege to silence the blood-crazed miscreations of American public life—those monsters alive in our judicial, education, economical, and political systems—intent on eating away at gains essential to a sustainable life together in a nation founded on a lie of White exceptionalism.

To breathe life into our imagination, we can explore new arrangements and experiences. Our hope for the truest realization of this world asks for us to unbridle our democratic expectations. It's high time to unleash the full power of our government by believing in what people want, stagnating partisanship, and legislating the impossible. Contrary to Otto von Bismark's characterization of politics as the art of the possible,[26] abolition is the art of the so-called impossible, the art of realizing the best thing. As we have explored throughout this work, we have an obligation to scrutinize racial thinking. We must create overwhelming global demands for thinking outside of white boxes.

Abolition is a form of analysis and organizing practice centered not on the systems that harm us but on the process of imagining repair, justice, and equality into being. We are attempting to make something, not just to erase something. Abolition is an existential reaching for the should-be and could-be by risking power and privilege. Abolition believes a sustainable future exists beyond the necessary destruction of the evil we've always known. The early abolitionists believed the nation first had to repent of its sin by ending slavery and then had to figure out what should be done in its place. Just because there is no exact, detailed, vivid blueprint for the future does not mean the insidious evils of structural dehumanization and disinheritance should not be dismantled immediately.

While we lack a comprehensive blueprint for the future, we can start with an unambiguous, clarion demand and an espousal of a faith in an unseen, unexperienced, and unprecedented social order. Frederick Douglass sobers us: "Power concedes nothing without a demand. It never did and it never will. . . . The limits of tyrants are prescribed by the endurance of those whom they oppress."[27] The implications of the *imago Dei* compel me to stop short of believing that those responsible for harm are incapable of being personally transformed into reparative intercessors. The contemporary custodians of our fatal status quo can be persuaded and undergo a renewing of their minds in favor of power-sharing and equity-building. However, there is no need to wait for such a realignment of life. Though these high-level concessions would lower some of the risks for the unprotected, an abolitionist vision turns on the will of vulnerable communities, not simply the will of the powerful.

Freedom enlists us to soberly stare down the atrocities that hold our fragile public life in place and nevertheless contribute to the mighty streams of change that undo our existing conditions. Upstream demands that overhaul institutions and structures require radical imagination and an ongoing belief that we can redirect massive capital toward big possibilities like universal housing, healthcare, job guarantees, and childcare.

Abolition calls for the end of private and public prisons that irrecoverably extract resources and people out of Black and Brown residential communities. Abolition demands "historically situated, racially relevant, culturally contextual, communally conscious"[28] teaching that advances the opportunities of Black and Latinx students as emerging voters and taxpayers. Abolition speaks up for a single-payer healthcare system that closes the racial health gap by providing free, high-quality services that address the disparities that contribute to lower Black and Latinx life expectancies and the underlying conditions that raised the COVID-19 fatality rate in the United States. Abolition communicates a need for investments in the economy like a federal job guarantee that mandates the US government to create and sustain high-wage employment for everyone who wants a job and while honoring the dignity of work and workers.

As an act of reconstruction, the pulse to risk causes us to ask:

- If I could do anything at all to end racism, what would I do?
- What could an anti-racist church look like?
- What would be the features of an anti-racist economy?
- What images, words, and ideas come to mind when I consider the following:
    sufficiency
    shared abundance
    liberation
    God/the sacred
    multiracial solidarity
    community

The pulse to risk, a vital embodiment of the spiritual life, compels us to sacrifice our power and privilege so consistently, intentionally, and freely that it no longer feels like a sacrifice but a sacrament. Risk-responsive faith in humanity expects and welcomes opposition as a pathway to societal re-creation, an occasion to unlock the power of human resilience sparked by our divinity—our *imago Dei*. This is true even when the opposition surfaces from within us. Abolitionist spirituality funds our risks, urging us to do something counterintuitive and self-sacrificial. The succor of our spirituality correlates to the amplitude of our resistance to the status quo. We must ask ourselves whether we have the stamina to give up nonparticipation, gradualism, comforts of norms, racial pessimism, and embedded thinking.

"I'm scared of the backlash."

6

Downbeat Truth

Naming Our Complicity in Racism

The first time I taught a Black Lives Matter course at New York Theological Seminary, the Supreme Court confirmation hearing for Judge Amy Coney Barrett commanded our attention. As an originalist, Barrett said, "I interpret the Constitution as a law. I understand it to have the meaning that it had at the time people ratified it. That meaning doesn't change over time, and it is not up to me to update it or infuse my policy views into it."[1] I must point out that the framers of the Constitution never considered Black citizenship and Black humanity. This judicial philosophy has been used to preserve slavery, uphold segregation, and gut voting rights.

As we outlined some of these concerns in class, one of the Black students asked, "Judge Amy has Black children from Haiti. How can she be racist? What's more anti-racist than raising Black children, Prof?"

Of course Judge Barrett loves her Black children as much as her White children. That's the wrong litmus test for anti-racism. Alongside her maternal love, her public record as a judge and scholar reeks of racism. No one is inherently racist; we inherit racist ideas, privileges, and practices. You can be racist and a good person—charitable, church-involved, altruistic, and loving toward Black friends and relatives. A person can be married to a Black person, birth and raise a Black person, and support Black-owned businesses while being racist. Anti-racism requires more than good intentions, strong individual relationships, and charitable actions. The infrastructure of Whiteness won't allow us to settle for being a friendly person who knows what racism is and how it is wrong. So far, every moment in this nation's history has cried out for people settled in their souls not to cooperate with our lethal drama of race.

Though a contested term, *allyship* is an ongoing practice of freedom that begs us to look beyond our relationships with and charitable acts toward persons from unprotected communities. By leveraging their privilege, allies serve as accomplices to abolition and equity alongside unprotected communities. Allyship is a consistent, selfless, and meticulous practice of solidarity with sinned-against communities by a person with some social privilege. This way of being means unlearning and relearning the nature of society and one's role in it. Simply put, a person who engages in allyship does the following:

- Deprioritizes their own needs
- Builds relationships with impacted persons
- Listens to the voices of sinned-against communities
- Embraces the meaning of allyship as defined and directed by impacted persons
- Resists saviorism
- Openly acknowledges complicity with oppression
- Owns the process of self-education

Each task explored in the preceding chapters speaks to the hallmarks of one's formation as a reparative intercessor. Reparative intercessors include the privileged and the impacted. This is the work of dying to and grieving Whiteness; divesting from mythic innocence; cultivating a posture of interracial, material interdependence; conquering veiled prejudices; and sacrificing power and privilege to form us into new beings. These rhythms are what constitute the vocation of reparative intercessors.

White noise tells us to avoid the distress of conversing about racism. Allies do the work of telling on themselves and anticipating backlash to initiate real social change from their kitchen tables and Sunday school rooms to the halls of Congress and the operating room. At the interface of the public and the personal, harvesting discomfort and embracing its power are first steps toward transformation. Racial idleness gives way to our abundant humanity when we face our fears of uncovering our racial incompetence, listen deeply to the othered when we are at a loss for words, and work hard to get our feelings out of the way so we can get in the way of racism.

When white noise compels us to avoid the diligence, emotional exhaustion, and retaliations involved with addressing racism, we can practice rhythm six, downbeat truth: harvesting the discomfort of telling on ourselves. When we engage in downbeat truth, we name our complicity with racism rather than feel scared of the backlash. We prefer not to live confronted by our racist tendencies, dissociated from family and childhood friends, or labeled a race-baiting radical, but we need to come to terms with the variables in our lives that stop us from unraveling the threads of racial hurt. We also tell on ourselves by owning our fidelity to racial repair. It should not be a secret that we invest ourselves in causes of the sinned against. The discomfort of telling on ourselves also exposes the complicity with White supremacy of others in our orbits. Reparative intercession invites backlash from uncircumspect people dying from Whiteness and the inner angst of naming how our past and present behaviors, thoughts, and speech perpetuate inequalities.

The theatrics of White guilt ring hollow for true social transformation. We have all seen these theatrics: crying, overtalking, rationalizing our experiences, paralyzing self-frustration, and ignoring impacted people. An example would be when some revelation of the horrors White people authored might get through the defenses of a White person and trigger tears before an audience of Black people. A White woman once confided in me her take on this: "They think if they've shown some remorse to a Black person that they are already proving how much they aren't racist." Unfortunately, these beneficiaries of White privilege have only caused more misery and work for the Black people enduring White people's fragility, insecurities, and self-interest.

White people must undertake the work of self-education regarding racial justice despite the discomfort. In some cases, it's as easy as performing a Google search or watching a YouTube video. Erin Samson, a White participant of Public Love Organizing and Training (PLOT), opined, "White people are used to being centered on and catered to. The thought of personal growth isn't appealing. I'm thinking that the months and years of unlearning what we've been taught is a slog we aren't interested in going through unless someone is clapping and telling us they think what we are doing is wonderful. So when they are reaching out to Black people, it isn't entirely for help; it is because they want credit for wanting help. It is a little bit of immediate absolution."

Personally, I long for the end of White credentialing on race. Credentialing consists of attempts by White people to show how woke they are: what anti-racism literature they have read, how many Black friends they have, what causes they support, and what courses they have taken. As an anti-racism facilitator for churches and public-school districts, I am regularly greeted by the usual litany of remarks:

- "I have Black friends."
- "I read Robin DeAngelo's *White Fragility*."

- "I took a diversity and inclusion class at work."
- "I am an ally; I hired a Black assistant."
- "I voted for Obama and Kamala."

Reaping the Fruit of Indifference

White noise perpetuates the goal of racism that ensures people say and do nothing. Howard Thurman posits, "To decide not to decide, is to decide against."[2] We decide against liberty when we do nothing. We decide against justice when we rinse our hands of the issue. We decide against democracy when we put our hands in our front pockets and walk away whistling in resignation to partisanship. We decide against humanness when we seal our lips at work and lunch.

Unborn generations cannot feed on the fruit of our indifference. Robert Kennedy once shared, "If we fail to dare, if we do not try, the next generation will harvest the fruit of our indifference; a world we did not want—a world we did not choose—but a world we could have made better, by caring more for the results of our labor."[3] Our stomachs turn at the taste of the rotten fruit of our past inactions. The decline in Black homeownership is the fruit of our indifference to greed-crazed capitalism after the crash of 2008. Our opioid crisis today is the fruit of our indifference toward Black people with substance dependence during the crack-ladened 1990s. The racial wealth gap today is the fruit of our indifference to calls for reparations since 1865. The police-involved killings of unarmed Black people is the fruit of our indifference to police brutality since the 1960s.

Though conservatives and White evangelicals are typically the first to be called out for hiding behind white noise, "liberals" also perpetuate systemic and individual Whiteness. Many penthouse progressives maintain a safe distance from impacted communities while majoring in laser-sharp analysis. Without a fresh animation of anti-racism by incarnational ethics, these do-gooders will forge ahead insulated by their privilege and untouched by the fruit of their inaction and idealistic theories.

Cheap approximations of solidarity—hashtags, retweets, donations, debates, and the like—assuage the feelings of liberals. More and more, would-be co-conspirators write "Black Lives Matter" and still segregate schools and communities. They shout, "Black Lives Matter," and still degrade the Black poor as inherently prone to criminal behaviors. They tweet, "Black Lives Matter," and blame victims of police brutality for their own deaths due to noncompliance. A nominal ally can lift Black Lives Matter signs and practice quietism while Latin American children languish in cages. Corporate donors can write checks to Black Lives Matter and refuse to hire Black women or even refuse to believe they deserve equal pay for work equivalent to that of White people and Black men.

Non-White interracial solidarity adds needed texture to the call to allyship, requiring the necessity for developing syncopated identity. Class and gender play a seismic role in how Black and Latinx folks serve as racial allies to the more vulnerable. It's possible to be oppressed and oppressive at the same time. You can be Black and middle class and demonize the poor; Black and male and perpetuate patriarchy; Black and American and discriminate against immigrants; Black and educated and abandon those already abandoned by public schools.

Dwell among Us: Allyship as Incarnation and Intercession

Risk-responsive solidarity in racial repair requires having some skin in the game. Long-distance, words-only commitments spread the mildewed fruit of indifference. True allyship blooms in the soil of our unity. The touchstones of intercession and incarnation elevate my approach to allyship to the level of a spiritual discipline as we anticipate and weather backlash. Put simply, reparative intercession rotates around the question, "Where and how are we willing to shred our hesitancies and show up for racial justice?"

Incarnation(s)

We are called to come alongside people who live beneath what the late Samuel DeWitt Proctor called the "scratch line."[4] Early on, incarnation proves fruitful for mining the tasks of solidarity, neighborliness, and allyship, speaking to its urgency and exigency. Incarnation localizes the divine in humanity without the divine losing its "everywhere-ness" and eternality. Here I do not intend to make a doctrinal claim about Jesus as an exception to the rule of humanity. I intend to present him as an exemplar of human potential. For me, incarnation speaks to the particularity of the divine in its limitless manifestations and the universality of its accessibility. Incarnation means to become human.

Incarnation as eternal allyship is manifested in a Palestinian carpenter under the full weight of the settler colonialism of Rome. Divinity crescendos in humanity through a spiritual genius who was pulled from the womb of an indigenous people who were enslaved in Egypt, migrated as landless nomads, were war-tossed by international exploiters, and were occupied by Assyrians, Babylonians, Persians, and Greeks. Jesus lived among the sinned against, unprotected, and exploited in the Roman Empire.

Against the backdrop of systemic sins that reinforce racial hierarchy, segregate, and dehumanize, we answer the call to be abundantly human with one another. Reparative intercession bids us to see incarnation as an ongoing phenomenon awaiting our participation. We practice the presence of God in our daily brushes with those who are unprotected in ways that widen the window for racial justice. We are reminded that the Spirit calls us to unfasten economic shackles and demolish gendered walls for Black and Brown people now, not in some abstract, distant, quasi-promised sweet by-and-by. A state-of-emergency, time-is-running-out mentality—characterized by police and vigilantes killing Black millennials, an expanding racial wealth gap, and a disproportionate number of Black and Latinx deaths due to COVID-19—tells us we cannot wait for political messiahs or a convenient moment.

While white noise hums sedative refrains like "There's nothing you can really do" and "You can't risk losing these comforts," the Spirit says, "If not you, then who? If not now, then when?" Practicing the presence of God—incarnation as allyship—costs us even as it advances us. Ultimately, White people benefit from the abolition of racial oppression as their souls are freed from the corrosiveness of Whiteness. The best possible outcome for White people emerges when they embrace interdependence with non-White people and see how the millions of poor middle-class and working-class people have been abandoned by the very economic hierarchy they aspire to ascend.

In his missive to the Philippians, Paul invoked a first-century hymn that amplifies the image of Jesus leveraging power and privilege as an incarnational act.

> Let each of you look not to your own interests, but to the interests of others. Let the same mind be in you that was in Christ Jesus, who, though he was in the form of God, did not regard equality with God as something to be exploited, but *emptied himself*, taking the form of a slave, being born in human likeness. And being found in human form, he humbled himself and became obedient to the point of death—even death on a cross. (2:4–8, emphasis added)

The call to embody the risk and potential of Jesus even makes its way into the Pauline corpus. According to the hymn's interpretation of Jesus's entry into time, Jesus identified his special privilege (equality with God), leveraged it to secure the promise of humanity (emptied himself), and braved the undue backlash (became obedient to the point of death). One interpreter identifies a nuance in the Greek translation: "*because* he was in the form of God, he did not regard equality with God as something to be exploited."[5] Jesus refused to exploit equality with God. Living out the form of God pivots on the practices of radical self-sacrifice and revolutionary self-investment when self-consumption and self-aggrandizement inflate the ethos of the day. Per this tradition, Jesus *emptied himself* to find solidarity with vulnerable humanity.

The Greek word for "empty" in the letter is *kenōsis*. It is in Jesus's self-emptying kenotic love that he reveals what God is like and what humanity must become. It is through assuming the lowest posture that we practice God's presence in an imbalanced world. Jesus emptied not in the sense of a loss of self but in the sense of pouring out his grace and goodness to God's creation. Through preaching and teaching, healing the sick, investing in the poor, reclining with sinners, and enduring a government-sponsored execution, Jesus poured out his life for the masses of the othered. When we live out an abolitionist spirituality, we learn that sustaining life together requires a self-emptying that allows us to find our abundant humanity. We must empty ourselves to fully find ourselves. Kenotic love allows us to walk in the manifestation of fresh power. It forges ground for us to stand on in the places of people with whom we must cocreate a new world. The future dangles on the fragile strings of our egos, social locations, and tenacious willingness to identify and use our power and privilege to advance life. The incarnational passions of reparative intercession force us to empty our privilege—male privilege, White privilege, citizenship privilege, economic privilege, and sexuality privilege, to name just a few.

One actionable example of emptying privilege is when White people work on other White people. After an anti-racism workshop that I facilitated in 2015, one participant recounted a moment when she realized she had cast a wide racist narrative due to an isolated experience with a Black person. She prefaced her story by naming a few racial moments that marked her childhood: (1) first learning about the Black poet Nikki Giovanni in sixth grade, (2) the first time she had a sleepover with a Black friend, (3) singing "Lift Every Voice and Sing" during assemblies in elementary school, and (4) a field trip to see Spike Lee's *Malcolm X* as a high school senior. She shared:

> From third to sixth grade, I was one of only a couple White kids in my class. Our principal was a Black woman. Seventh through twelfth grade, I attended a school that was majority White. We had Black teachers, including Sharon Draper, who went on to become an extremely successful young adult author. However, conversations about race did not happen in our household. In fact, I only remember one, and that was between me and my father.
>
> My father has one sister. When she was barely out of her teens, she married a Black man from a tough neighborhood in Chicago named Frank. He was not a good person, and the marriage got very bad very quickly. My aunt left him, and he shot her in the back. The surgery to remove the bullet damaged her spine, and she was left paralyzed.
>
> My sister started dating a Black boy from a low-income housing development while we were in high school. He was very nice, and my parents seemed to like him. I knew my aunt's story, though, and thought it surely must affect their feelings. I am not proud to share what I said to my father: "I would understand if you didn't want your daughter to date a Black person from a bad neighborhood." My father shook his head and said, "Frank was one person." I know there was more to the conversation, but I also know that that one sentence was everything. I learned in that moment that it's ludicrous to hate or blame an entire group of people for the actions of one person just because they share skin color.

Nearly thirty years later, that conversation with her father has germinated a pledge to challenge her racism and privilege. She concluded, "I needed to learn about racism from my family and friends for it to stick with me. Sometimes conversations will be painful, and oftentimes they will feel fruitless. However, none of these are reasons not to have them." Though I believe racism merits explicit naming, her White father hushed her white noise without explicitly calling her a racist, scolding her harshly, or raising his voice beyond a conversational tone. The woman's story illustrates the promise of intra-White conversations about racism. White people need to remember that dinner table talk, Sunday school discussions, and break room conversations matter profoundly to the work of racial repair.

Because White people rarely tell on themselves, the burden to generate even minimal change in White people habitually falls in the laps of non-White survivors of racism. Non-White people will give White people a pass on their daily racism in hopes of avoiding conflict, salvaging their careers and reputations, or saving their physical lives. It's not the job of non-White people to save White people from their power and privilege. We must all confront social forces to save ourselves from the racism that ravishes non-White life.

Self-advocacy and allyship rarely emerge without the threat of termination or toxic labeling. Denise, a Black trans woman, enjoyed a well-paying career in journalism prior to pursuing her vocation as a Christian minister. On November 5, 2008, the day after the historic election of Barack Hussein Obama to the US presidency, Denise entered the Metro Station in DC to board a train en route to the National Press Building. Not quite allowing herself to inhale the excitement surrounding the first Black president, she grabbed a copy of the *New York Times* and a cup of coffee—a daily routine.

When she arrived at the office, she stored her resources and turned on her computer. Oddly, she noticed virtually no one was in the front of the office. With her coffee in hand and an eagerness to revel in the Obama victory, she headed toward the executive offices in the rear of the complex. The entire sales team was there eating breakfast around a computer screen and laughing.

At first, her coworkers failed to notice she had entered the room. She assumed the laughter and congregating were part of an enthusiasm that their guy had won! An awkwardness fell over the space as she greeted everyone. They each said good morning with some reticence. When Denise asked the reason behind the laughter, her coworkers walked away in an eerie silence, embarrassingly bowing their heads. One coworker responded, "You wouldn't think it's funny, Denise." She jovially replied, "Yes, I will." He revealed that they were laughing at a caricature of president-elect Obama holding a bucket of chicken in one hand and a watermelon in the other. The caption read, "Weez in dah big house now!" Denise reflected to me, "I said nothing, because I did not realize I had options. It sounds silly, but it's true. I didn't realize that there are numerous ways one can respond to racism at work. I stood there with a sense of powerlessness."

Denise's reaction mirrors my own in similar situations. Most non-White people disengage in such scenarios because of the clear imbalance of power and the standardization of Black and Brown disposability. White reparative intercessors must learn the balance between participation and presence short of succumbing to the seductions of saviorism. Self-emptying as a path to abundant humanity and solidarity is important so as not to make racial justice about massaging egos and emotions. Risking power and privilege is a refusal to cooperate with the way things have been. Mahatma Gandhi asserted, "Non-co-operation is not a passive state, it is an intensively active state, more active than physical resistance or violence. Passive resistance is a misnomer. Non-co-operation in the sense used by me must be non-violent and therefore, neither punitive nor based on malice, ill-will or hatred."[6] Abolition urges a new configuration of the present order and a radical divestment from it. Presence and participation alongside impacted persons and allies looks like noncooperation with the sins of Whiteness, including transmuting oneself into the hero of the moment.

In 2018, I facilitated a workshop on effective allyship and the roles of faith communities in dismantling mass incarceration with a largely White audience at the national summit of the New Baptist Covenant. Founded by former US president Jimmy Carter, New Baptist Covenant engages in cross-racial community service and justice projects undertaken by local congregations. By design, between the annual summits, the organization encourages Black and White Baptist churches to pair up for fellowship and service. Most of the non-clergy attendees worship at churches that serve as Covenant partners, which are the congregations committed to building cross-racial relationships and fulfilling Covenant of Action projects. The actions range from developing literacy programs to advocating against predatory lending.

I arrived in Atlanta expecting to meet White Christians devoted to social justice as a cardinal feature of faith. During the sessions, I slowed the conversation down to emphasize the need to discard White saviorism—the largely unspoken conviction that non-White people need White people's charitable involvement. "A White savior impairs the work of justice," I said.

During the question-and-answer time, one of the learners shared about the mentorship program established by her church and a Black church in her city and concluded, "We are saving *those* young people from the streets."

"Not saving. That's not justice," another White attendee belted out.

The internalized savior complex is about having a big emotional experience. White saviorism—and non-White middle-class saviorism—settles for the emotional ease of parachuting into "the hood" and low-wealth communities for a couple hours. Reparative intercession, instead, has a vested interest in racial mutuality that guards against any air of saviorism. True racial justice cannot advance on sympathy and charity alone.

Kenotic love—self-emptying love—propositions us, after more than four hundred years of Blacks and poor Whites existing in America as social throwaways and political piñatas, to pour ourselves into this moment of cultural scapegoating to create a movement of love, into political peril to create possibilities of economic sustainability, into the growing social anxiety to create new linkages of belonging, and into this existential hell to be visible reminders of hope.

Intercession(s)

Intercession points to an in-between place. Remember the image of standing in the tragic gap introduced at the beginning of this book. The downbeat truth of reparative intercession is an expectation to invest in a life of perpetual becoming always shy of reaching full realization. Allyship is a middle passage we know we may never row out of but still we continue to paddle against the current. We will never be anti-racist even as we sustain our anti-racist work and increase cross-racial relationships. The symbol of intercession, in a sense, reorients us to find sufficiency and energy in the doing and becoming, not in the destination or moniker. Maybe this gives some context to what Jesus meant by "My food is to do the will of the one who sent me" (John 4:34).

A White assistant principal in a majority-White school helped me parse some of the land mines of intercession and saviorism. He relayed the following story to me:

A Latina eighth grade girl was having difficulty with a White male teacher. He often wrote her up for talking back, or getting angry, or walking out of the classroom. She and I would talk about their conflicts, and she told me that he picked on her. I believed the true story was somewhere in the middle. It got to the point where she would sometimes come to my office just to take a breath before going to the class, even though I assigned a couple of lunch and after school detentions related to interactions with the teacher. The teacher told me that the mom "didn't care" and was never home to take care of her kids or the situation.

One day after the student walked out of class to come to my office, I called her mom and told her about the ongoing conflict with the teacher, thinking I was telling her something she didn't know. She shared her own distress over the situation. She said she leaves for work before her daughter wakes up in the morning, but she calls her on her way to school every morning to talk through how she could stay calm if the teacher said something that day. They also talked about it at dinner every night. So here I was giving myself credit for helping her regulate her emotions when her mom was teaching her every day how to navigate a racist situation and racist people with authority over her. Mom's grace in not blaming this situation on me or the teacher filled me with shame. I hung up with her and said out loud to myself, "Who the hell do I think I am?" I return to that pain often because I know sitting in it makes me better. And frequently asking myself that same question both humbles me and gives me resolve.

Only after resolving that a person's interpretation of their lived experience is credible will we be able to walk alongside them with compassion and caring. Standing in the gap for a person—the work of *intercession*—means we believe people's experiences. Being present for a person—the work of *incarnation*—means we believe people's testimonies about life. Reparative intercessors believe Black people. Reparative intercessors believe Latinx people. Reparative intercessors believe Asian people. Reparative intercessors believe non-White women. Reparative intercessors believe non-White queer people.

Reparative intercession positions us to breathe together, not for each other. Allyship is the death of paternalism, co-opting, mansplaining, and Whitesplaining. We conspire to remodel our fragile world. Literally, conspire means to "breathe together" (from the Latin *con* meaning "with" and *spire* meaning "breathe"). The privileged and the disadvantaged breathe together the same air of resistance, reimagination, and reconstruction. A divine conspiracy of abolition—a breath from God—restores the dream of an America that prizes racial equity in our politics, economics, schools, and healthcare.

One unseasonably warm February weekend, I visited Savannah, Georgia, for the first time while speaking at a men's retreat. I toured the oldest independent Black church in the United States: the First African Baptist Church. First African was used as a stop along the Underground Railroad. For the safety of all involved, no records were kept of how many slaves found refuge at this church on their way to the North. The ceiling of the church is designed with what is called a Nine Patch Quilt, which signified to the runaways that this was a place of resting and safety. Of course, it was a hidden signal that only certain people knew about. Most people would have thought the Nine Patch Quilt was simply a beautiful design in a church ceiling.

To gain entry into the area of the church connected to the Underground Railroad, slaves entered through a tunnel, which stretched to the river or one of the neighboring structures. I was captured by the holes in the floor in certain areas of the church. These holes are arranged in a pattern known as a Bakongo Cosmogram—an African worship symbol. I loved the fact that the church installed these holes in the floor to allow the slaves beneath the floorboards to breathe. Using our power and privilege amid traumatic, tragic, and terrifying racial crises, in a sense, gives breathing room to the unprotected.

Loyalty to Loyalty

Intercessory and incarnational practices pivot on breathing together, emptying egos of pretention, and placing ourselves alongside the unprotected. Intercession and incarnation arise from a loyalty beyond the self—loyalty as an ethical and spiritual principle. To what are we loyal? Josiah Royce, a philosopher, challenges us to reassess the nerve center of our lives, to find a way of being greater than the flinching of our egos due to self-centeredness. For Royce, loyalty is "the willing and practical and thoroughgoing devotion of a person to a *cause*."[7] Loyalty to a cause is palpably self-initiated, actionable, other-centered, and communal. This is a way of telling on ourselves as devotees to agendas larger than our individual concerns and projects that advance the telos—the purpose—of humanity.

A good cause is always a social enterprise that binds humanity "into the unity of one service." It involves being loyal to the greatest amount of flourishing for all. Royce posits, "A cause is good, not only for me, but for [hu]mankind, in so far as it is essentially a *loyalty to loyalty*, that is, is an aid and furtherance of loyalty in my fellows."[8] Loyalty to loyalty guides our contribution to causes that represent the greatest good for humanity and recruits more faithfulness to the same. The downbeat truth is that we shrink in front of those who need our reparative intercessory action because the act forces us to shelve our immediate individual benefits and entreats us to center our appreciations and energies on the othered. But life can only be truly lived interpersonally. We find that the grace of life—the self-giving hope that enriches the othered—is experienced only in loving community.

Loyalty to loyalty finds its character in the dual embodiment of justice and benevolence. I equate loyalty to anti-racism as a loyalty to humanity because it is a high good, not simply because it is winnable, immanent, or faddish. When we live surrendered to a God-cause, "defeat, disappointment, failure, and sorrow ought each to be seen as 'a positive aid to loyalty.'"[9] The perpetual in-betweenness of reparative intercession pressures us to see the paradox of loyalty. Like faith, loyalty dares people to fail when the cause grows us the public good. Loyalty to a specific cause ought to produce greater loyalty in humanity and contribute to the good of humanity as a whole. Anti-racism must become one with our very lives like a slow-growing, airborne "contagion." Though a narrow, special cause, reparative intercession reflects loyalty to humanity with robust interface with anti-sexist, anti-classist, anti-homophobic loyalties. These loyalties ought to inspire each other toward loyalty to humanity.

When we do not manage to see beyond self-interest, we futilely pledge our fealty to cloths and fabric arranged in stars and stripes, to documents whose framers segregated their ideals, to traditions designed to control the humanity of the powerless, and to sacrosanct symbols that reinforce racial hierarchy. Genuine loyalty transcends our nominal commitments to brick and mortar, parchment, and personalities. The future of our lives together obligates faithfulness to causes that renovate the very structures of society and the structures of our awareness. Self-evasive and self-centered behaviors make it exceedingly difficult to assess the world-making consequences that our actions and inaction bring into being. Directly and unwittingly, we influence the inner and material lives of real persons. Does our loyalty lend itself to the cultivation of a more just, inclusive, power-sharing, sustainable world?

As part of an incarnational lifestyle, loyalty to anti-racism obligates that we deploy our bodies in some way to disrupt the continuum of injustice and discrimination. Loyalty transcends our hollow verbal commitments and doctrinal formulations, mandating actions that align with our professions. This work reflects an actionable commitment to life-making, community-expanding, spirit-nourishing ideals. Reparative intercessors see their mental, spiritual, and material commitments to racial justice as loyalty to humanity—a loyalty to loyalty conspired with the divine. Racism exemplifies an extreme disloyalty to humanity and harms both the violators and the violated. An expression of loyalty to loyalty, reparative intercession is a call to be resolutely faithful to justice, forgiveness, charitability, grace, community, peace, equality, reparation, freedom, truth, and truth-telling.

Why loyalty to anything bigger than oneself? Loyalty to the "mystery of loving membership in a community whose meaning seems divine" can transform the individual.[10] This transformation represents vast possibilities for our society. Loyalty to racial justice transforms the privilege of White people into a resource to dismantle the daily enmeshed forms of racism that so painfully operate beneath the radar. Loyalty to racial justice transforms the class privilege of some Black and Latinx people into opportunities to castigate the economic incentives of Whiteness. "Reverberating all through you, stirring you to your depths, loyalty first unifies your plan of life, and thereby gives you what nothing else can give—[that is to say] your Self as a life lived in accordance with a plan, your conscience as your plan interpreted for you through your ideal, your cause as your personal purpose in living."[11] Loyalty impresses meaning into our existence, forging a way for real life.

A Profile in Reparative Intercession

History previews the myriad daunting and discomforting demands of loyalty to racial justice. In our contemporary iteration of this racial dilemma, we question the feasibility of multiracial solidarity and divestment from privilege. William Lloyd Garrison—a White New England abolitionist—offers us an exceptional profile in reparative intercession that emboldens the call for immediate, intersectional, individual, and institutional change. Garrison bridges the gap between abolitionist spirituality and White allyship. The unorthodox and predictably unpopular faith leader threw his influence as a White man into play, anticipated and welcomed White retaliation, and embodied loyalty to the cause of abolition. Among so many other White abolitionists in the Black-led movement, Garrison epitomizes the tenacious values that make for fruitful anti-racist allyship.

Contesting and repositioning his White male privilege, the freedom fighter vehemently criticized the Americanized forms of Christianity and the civic rites and structures that upheld race-based slavery in this nation. His thirty-five years of editorial service to *The Liberator* and his demand for immediatism—the instant abolition of slavery and equal rights for free and freed Black people—brought him to blows with the American political establishment, White propertied men, and more moderate abolitionists. Garrison's abolitionist vision challenged his evangelical identity, expanded the public policy conversation, and appealed to a multiracial audience of public agitators. One Independence Day, he publicly burned a copy of the US Constitution—as an act of conscientious citizenship—to show the heights of his resistance to unjust laws. Many evangelical clergy and moderate abolitionists accused the editor of hurting the work of abolition with his nonconformist behavior.[12]

Garrison teaches us to work intersectionally. Early on in his leadership in the broad-based, largely Black-led abolition movement, Garrison advanced debates related to women's leadership in the movement and membership in the American Anti-slavery Society while regularly supporting the organizing and writing of woman suffragists. Several influential Boston abolitionists distanced themselves from Garrison's work and the Massachusetts Anti-slavery Society over the question of the status of women.[13] In 1840, he recalcitrantly staged a walkout and boycott at the first international antislavery convention in London due to its exclusion of women delegates.

Backlash is a part of the cost of allyship—our enfleshment. It is one of the ways we pay for being free and expanding freedom to all. It is constitutive of the story my body tells of power sharing, radical humility, or privilege-leveraging presence. In addition to the emotional toll and bodily exhaustion native to the work of justice, Garrison endured incarceration, alienation, being dragged through the streets of Boston, being nearly lynched after a meeting at Faneuil Hall, and losing revenue for his publication due to his reparative intercession during the long night of chattel slavery. His opposition to the White sin of slavery demanded he leverage his White privilege for the chained humanity of enslaved Africans. He emptied himself in the fight for freedom and equity—showing his loyalty to loyalty.

I'm Not There Yet: Intercessor Interrogatives

I have found it quite healthy to regularly put myself through rigorous self-interrogation. Self-interrogation stops us from merely checking boxes and patting ourselves on the back for the good we do for "them" "over there." Reparative intercessors ask discomforting questions to ensure they can show up, speak up, and act up on behalf of the other. You might ask yourself:

- To what am I loyal? Why? How does it advance humanity?
- Do I know any racial justice allies?
- Who have I been formed to love?
- Who have I been conditioned to see as my neighbor?
- What is forming me? How am I reforming those influences?
- What am I sacrificing to build racial justice?
- How can I continue to learn about racial equity and repair today?
- What is my best possibility for learning from Black and other non-White people?
- What took me so long to get here?
- What types of support do I need?
- What aspects of my identity are privileged? (Race? Class? Gender? Sexuality? Mental/Bodily Ability? Citizenship?)
- What aspects of my identity are marginalized? (Race? Class? Gender? Sexuality? Mental/Bodily Ability? Citizenship?)
- What barriers do I anticipate?
- What am I willing to give up?
- What, if anything, about this journey causes me fear?
- When have I taken a risk for racial repair and justice?
- What was the last occasion presented to me to practice reparative intercession?
- Have I missed an opportunity to confront racism recently?
- How can I show up authentically to the fight?

CONCLUSION

Invent Hope Every Day

A week before my copy of Eddie Glaude's *Begin Again: James Baldwin's America and Its Urgent Lessons for Our Own* arrived, I hustled to create space in my calendar to watch an online conversation on YouTube between Glaude and his mentor, Cornel West. My love for James Baldwin as an artist and literary activist only grew after watching the wholehearted exchange between student and teacher. Their handling of Baldwin's biography invited me more deeply into his well of work. I sat transfixed by the conversation as Baldwin's words breathed life into my pandemic-fatigued soul. As an activist, I had felt hope for change slip away even as the US streets blazed with the glory of people peacefully and lawfully resisting the police state. The weighty tsunami of slayings that claimed the lives of Ahmaud Arbery, George Floyd, and Breonna Taylor in 2020 sent me into a fit of pessimism.

The single moment that owned me and resuscitated my prophetic imagination—my vision that America can be America—came when Glaude recounted an interview Baldwin gave to *Ebony* magazine in 1970. During one of Baldwin's exoduses from the shameful terror of the United States, the reporter from *Ebony* met him in Istanbul. At one point, the interviewer asked Baldwin, "What, then, about hope?" Baldwin, not terribly long removed from his own wrestling with suicide, answered, "Hope is invented every day."[1] Every day. That is it. We must invent hope every day. A great deal of what I love about Baldwin's spirituality spilled over in that single exchange.

As long as I draw breath on this earth, I will cherish those words that make my advocacy possible. Hope never just happens or emerges from some far side of the universe. We invent hope ourselves by working beyond the boundary lines of our comforts and privileges. We invent hope every day that we decide to take the trail down roads less traveled to repair the heart of a republic founded on the language of freedom and the practices of exploitation. I logged off for the remainder of that evening, affirming myself as a product of that day's hope invention. In fact, that broadcast invented hope for me that day.

Reparative intercession is a daily practice. It is a practice of inventing hope every day. The type of incarnational intercession championed in the preceding pages will help us invent hope for racial equity and Black freedom.

What about Hope?

Life grows increasingly easy to despair. The destabilizing horror of our silence and the caustic consequences of racism signal, in fever-pitch patriotic fervor, the end of what we claim to hold so dear. The soul of the United States stares at the gates of hell as Whiteness calls us by name. In 1916, in *Love for the Battle-torn Peoples*, Jenkin Lloyd Jones challenged, "No outside foe can ever denude this country, however much they may wish to storm our shores with shells or sink our battleships." He continued, "Nations do not die from invasion, they die from internal rottenness."[2] No nation that abandons the poor, stigmatizes the non-White, and conspires to create permanent underclasses will ultimately survive the free-flowing rhythm of time. The internal rottenness of mass incarceration, zip code injustice, poverty wages, the caging of Central American children at the southern border, and voter disenfranchisement attacks the nation-state at a cellular level as a metastasizing moral cancer. Unchecked structural injustice accelerates the demise of a nation irrespective of the nation's military prowess, economic superiority, and technological innovation. We look around and falsely believe that soaring skyscrapers, money-loaded politics, or Hollywood productions will last forever in spite of the ways we strip others of their rights. The structural sins of this democracy—the internal rottenness—infect and supplant our highest ideals, stored away in our libraries, artifacts, and monuments.

I judge America so harshly not as an unpatriotic agitator or some unhinged anarchist. My love for democracy and freedom, humanity and God instructs me to belt out clarion cries for national transformation. I rebuke my country's practices of tyranny and hierarchy in light of its well-documented professions of justice, equality, and freedom of all. Today is the day for America and Americans to live up to the print version of themselves, the nation promised to the world on fragile pieces of parchment. It appears our national experiment with democracy may prove to be more fragile than those aged pieces of paper.

We can no longer substitute the myth of America for the facts of our tormented racial experience. We hoped the devastating outcomes during the COVID-19 pandemic and the ongoing pandemic of racialized violence could slap us out of our slumber. However, the moment amounted to little more than tenuous optimism. Despair is happening everywhere. Rage is happening everywhere. Death is happening everywhere. To be Black in America is to become hauntingly familiar with the idea of your own death. However, irrespective of our skin, we all live behind the tall walls of sin known as segregation, mass incarceration, and healthcare apartheid.

It is hard to muster hope against the backdrop of life-breaking, person-impairing, place-making racism. Hopelessness knocks on the doors of all but with a particular vengeance for those living on the underside of American power. Cornel West avers, "Nihilism . . . it is, far more, the lived experience of coping with a life of horrifying meaninglessness, hopelessness, and (most important) lovelessness."[3] Hopelessness, a life unmotivated by the prospects of God's presence, shatters us to the point that we lack the will and wisdom to re-member ourselves. Most of our lives flutter out of control when the forces of death allied with racism absurdly emerge each day. We expend time pacing the floor; we waste energy worrying ourselves into nameless graves shoveled by loveless people; we unconsciously collapse into fruitlessness when we stare blankly into defeat; we cower in corners of resignation incompatible with the promise of life etched into our hearts. Hopelessness empties any person of their vital inventory of the unseen—peace, creativity, imagination, love, and joy. Hopelessness is the oldest mortuary of true living—an undertaker of the highest caliber. We drag around hopelessness, slowing our progress, impacting our direction, cooling our momentum, and blocking our creativity.

What about hope? Hope as an Americanized ideal and bourgeois shell of optimism fans the perpetuation of "good" for those in power, and a perpetuation of suffering for victims of our racially divided history. The naive optimism we attempt to pass off as hope serves the interests of people who play dice with our well-being and benefit from our powerlessness. The hope-deluded persons pining for social acceptance within a social schema structured against them believe progress rolls in on the wheels of inevitability. The chronic nature of Black pain on White crosses problematizes Martin Luther King Jr.'s audacious assertion that "the arc of the moral universe is long, but it bends toward justice."[4] All too often, anemic hope proxies as an excuse not to deal with the realities of injustice and the disintegration of flesh-and-blood feeling and breathing. For those struggling to survive, the truth remains that destitution and death await so many they love—and even themselves. In a very real sense, waiting leaves wide the gates of an arresting meaninglessness and nothingness.

We need a new version of hope, one that forges practices for engaging paralyzing challenges, uncomfortable exchanges, intense ideas, and the expectation of and stamina for progressive transformation. This hope is not a thin optimism. It registers more like blues hope, gritty hope. A blues hope honors the complexity of human personality, engagement, and existence. James Cone purports, "The blues are despair only in the sense that there is no attempt to cover up reality. . . . This hope provided the strength to survive, and also openness to the intensities of life's pains without being destroyed by them."[5] Somewhere I heard this articulated as hope on the downbeat of life.

Blues hope is the only hope I know in the world of abolition and repair. Blues hope utilizes the power of outrage and courage. According to Ralph Ellison, the blues sensation is "an impulse to keep the painful details and episodes of a brutal experience alive in one's aching consciousness, to finger its jagged grain, and to transcend it."[6] Blues hope is an enduring capacity to survive the tragic every day. With gritty hope, the people of God claim the power to name, lean into, and then transcend the tragic character of life together.

Be Hope

One of art's responsibilities is to attend to the burden of real suffering. Several years ago, I saw an arresting painting by Samuel Bak, a Holocaust survivor, at the Holocaust Museum in Houston while I was home visiting my mother. I pined for the prospect of entering Black History Month living in the costly intercession and solidarity of justice for all with its reminders of how we live stitched into a single garment of destiny that is exceedingly delicate. Bak's "Act of Balance" depicted an interpretation of hope—that is, blood-soaked, sturdy hope, not blind, whimsical optimism.[7] On one side of the ruins shown in his painting was the word *hope* stacked on top of block letters that make up the word *hope*, and on the other side, a man sat holding a sign with the word *hope*. A seemingly heavy cluster of wrecked hopes, in dark colors, on one side and a nondescript man holding a banner of hope on the other side were suspended over some images of ruin and devastation. Both sides remained balanced—by hope on one side and a man with hope on the other side. Hope did not fall because the man was on one side. He did not fall because hope was on the other side. Something is balanced only when it is equal on both sides. Hope sits on the other side of ruin, disorder, and turmoil and refuses to succumb to their gravitational pull. The man was equal to hope. You are equal to hope. We are equal to hope. We are the hope we need, the hope the world needs. We are the hope for change, hope for love, hope for peace, hope for a future. In the defeatist and disorienting throes of White racism, hope keeps the balance when racism threatens to tip life in the direction of economic precarity, floor us through political exclusion, or unsteady us in a bout of White cultural insecurities. We cannot fail or fall because we are equal to hope.

Everyday forms of resistance harvest power from below, a tactic to break apart the systems of meaning and truth historically produced by the ruling class. Every person is shaped by the discourse of White supremacy, which is important for analyzing the omnipresence of Whiteness and a perceived omnipotence of White power. Whiteness is neither simply about institutions nor simply about individuals; it is the name attributed to a complicated strategical situation that works beneath the consciousness of the individual and the machinations of our institutions. Therefore, white noise—particularly its doctrines and discourses that discipline us—demands urgent, consistent action from the unprotected and the privileged alike to realize racial repair. Michel Foucault contends, "Where there is power, there is resistance. . . . These points of resistance are present everywhere in the power network."[8] Such a diffuse notion about Whiteness also democratizes the potential for resistance. Microphysics of power—the subversive ways we act and speak in a larger system of relations—can disrupt the underside of all we have ever known legally, politically, and economically.

Hope probably remains flat on this page when some of us consider strategies for disrupting all forms of racism as well as their matrimony to all other oppressions. Still, I hope *hope* jumps off the page as a form of tactical resistance. Michel de Certeau, in *The Practice of Everyday Life*, asserts that strategies are actions available to persons privileged by power regimes, privileged with a sense of social power and privilege.[9] In contrast to a strategy, "a tactic is a calculated action determined by the absence of a proper locus. . . . The space of a tactic is the space of the other. Thus it must play on and with a terrain imposed on it. . . . It is a maneuver 'within the enemy's field of vision,' . . . and within enemy territory."[10] Though I categorically reject the conception of people as enemies, tactics belong to the other, to the marginalized. There is some otherness in the vast majority of all of us. Practices that evoke tactical resistance utilize people's otherness, allowing them to assert their subjectivity, humanity, and agency for the sake of new meanings, new stories, new interactions, and new witnesses. Tactical practices "manipulate the mechanisms of discipline and conform to them only in order to evade them." Depending on time and opportunities, tactical resistance "operates in isolated actions, blow by blow. . . . What it wins it cannot keep."[11] Tactics are transitory moments of subversion. Therefore, hope as a tactic of abolitionist spirituality undergirds reparative intercession. Every day we take refuge in the invention of hope as we delight in "the blow by blow," knowing tomorrow when we practice resistance on repeat that racism will stand a little weaker than the previous day.

Consistency is the only way to neutralize white noise and invent hope. The hope that keeps reparative intercessors engaged and supports their underlying spirituality is part of a ministry of erosion, which is a wearing down of structural evil—those arbiters of White sin that manifest in idolatry, the demonic, and segregation. As reparative intercessors, we throw ourselves into the sacred practice of consistent socially conscious presence, persistent neighborliness that wears down forces of destruction and corruption, structural evil, and organized sin. After the late-night killing of Breonna Taylor in her home, I witnessed and *hopefully* aided hope on a trip to Kentucky to attend a demonstration against police brutality and nonaccountability. I landed in Louisville with a heart ladened with grief and a mind trained on embodying resistance. I grieved the normalcy of police officers killing with impunity. I grieved that White supremacy demanded I leave home amid a merciless COVID-19 pandemic to stand in solidarity with protesters because "the system" continued to suffocate justice five and a half months after her murder.

As millennials crowded Cardinal Bridge and were hauled off and packed into jails in Louisville, they practiced hope, demanding the immediate arrest and prosecution of the murderers of Breonna Taylor. From DC to Los Angeles, people decried the murder of Breonna, George Floyd, and others every week for three consecutive months. Those multiracial, multigenerational troops embodied hope, wearing down evil one step, chant, or sign at a time. You can wake up every day with a stubborn resilience to show up and enflesh love in the face of grotesque, generations-deep, racist opposition.

The actions advocated in this book invite White people—and too-long-silent non-White people—into hope-inspired erosion: the work of eroding injustice and repairing lives devastated by racism. Our integrity hinges on our power to talk repair and then to live it out loud. Hope springs eternal the more presumed custodians of power understand that Black and Latinx people should lead, and they trust and believe them.

Hope takes courage and faith, given the long career of Whiteness. Without sacrificing its immediacy and urgency, reparative intercession curiously promotes revolutionary patience, which requires keeping our integrity even when the rest of the world seems to be splintering and cowering, stagnating and corrupting, scapegoating and caving. We fiercely refuse to surrender to the toxicity of the present, feed the stamina to keep working, and unimpeachably believe that transformation is underway. I am persuaded that hope guards us from being lulled to sleep by the jarring details we see and that it buttresses the resolve that tomorrow is breaking into today.

Our Souls Gotta Have It

We must save the soul of America because our souls and bodies depend on it. Jesus the abolitionist outlined in that Palestinian synagogue, as told in the fourth chapter of Luke, that spirituality is what we do on behalf of and with the unprotected. Thomas Merton, the highly reputed Trappist monk, cautions the faithful that the soul locates itself in bodily actions. The inner self, the true self, sees itself in "the mirror of its own activity."[12] We must act to avoid the inner death produced by inactivity and silence. Our doing acts on the soul, and the soul acts on the world. Abolitionist spirituality calls for coexistence, cocreation, and cogovernance as we live as persistent neighbors in sustainable ways. It is voluntary—we can choose to lean into the process.

You can begin to give yourself over to the rhythms of reparative intercession today. Use *cues to color* as a morning act of honesty as your feet meet the hardwood floor or warm carpet when you get out of bed. Paul *is* Black, Stephanie *is* Mexican, and Grace *is* Korean. Their race matters because it impacts their experiences in our streets and courtrooms. By daily acknowledging this palpably unavoidable facet, White people free themselves to celebrate the ineffable splendor of difference and healthily grieve a long-term relationship to racism that causes them to hold on to the lie that we all have the same opportunities.

Every day history walks beside us, and it behooves us to flow into the growing *momentum to encounter* the history that makes the present feel unquestionably natural. Mass non-White disparities owe a booming debt to twenty generations of White policy. The task remains to topple the pain-laced practices of racism today by recalling daily that long stories live behind these practices. It is a tall order to investigate and tell a history that robs us of our innocence without drowning in it, but it must be done.

In the previous chapters, I hope I underscored that Black and Latinx communities never lived alone under the onslaught of Whiteness. *Pattern recognition* allows us to see that Whiteness has a history of excluding, killing, and disenfranchising a great mass of White lives—namely, women and poor White people. Whiteness does more than erode the souls of White people; it abandons so many of them in service of the superrich and overprivileged. This tiny detail keeps me grounded in my rage, forcing me to see patterns that overwhelmingly bind us together.

A *syncopated identity* enables us to see living intersections within and around us. We silence white noise when we finger our places in the unyielding drama of oppression. The racial justice cause is an invitation to own all our identities—the marginalized and privileged selves that make each of us the person we are—and to see the same in others. New stories beat back, very slowly indeed, the stories of inferiority and superiority, fear and avoidance, and the hate and hurt we have known our whole lives. Every day we can find a new story of self to impact the now.

The *pulse to risk* is a sign that the work is alive; we are alive. The heart of the work is the will to risk power and privilege, which makes a new us and a better United States possible. That's the *downbeat truth* of this work. We will gain the thoroughly multiracial world of our imaginative energies only by being willing to give up power and privilege. Our words are not worth the dirt on which we walk without the endangering, sacrificial work of showing up. Sunday to Saturday we must be our words made flesh, thus daring to be God's word made flesh. We don't need another Martin Luther King Jr. or Fannie Lou Hamer, William Lloyd Garrison or Grimké sister. The moment is yours; it's ours.

If we abandon racial justice, we abandon God. If we abandon the impetus to repair and re-create, we give up on God when we truly need to give up power and privilege, comfort and silence. The appeal to invent hope daily infers the exasperating reality that hope is expiring every day. The private home and the public square emerge daily as the laboratories where we experiment with healthy cocktails that invent hope. Because God adores our freedom, prisons and detention centers become hope laboratories when we show up and demand their humane restructuring. Because God breathes the possibility of justice, public schools function as hope laboratories when we volunteer as emotional and academic resources for Brown and Black students left in segregated ruins. Because God consecrates unprecedented inclusion, our polling stations act as hope laboratories when we vote in the interest of expanding political freedoms, participation, and protections for non-White people. Our cubicle-arranged office spaces break through as hope laboratories when White people organize listening sessions and collective book readings addressing race for other White people. The Holy advises us to incarnate love, making our churches hope laboratories when Black, Latinx, and White people of faith co-labor to thwart the proliferation of state-sponsored deaths in our metropolitan communities. A hope durable enough to withstand daily assaults to racial justice and bolster our resolve to win asks us to go out of our way to see every space as a laboratory of hope.

Do we want to see our churches stronger, nation better, and communities harmonized? Do we want to see more children receive stellar educations and become contributing members of our society? Do we want to see the kin-dom of God on earth as it is in heaven? I believe our collective answer resounds yes. Our shared yes is louder than the white noise. I believe we want to do better and we shall.

I think we can change ourselves and the public if we do something anti-racist every day as an enfleshment of hope. We are not helplessly at the mercy of our political institutions, economic organizations, or impulses. If we face it all with courage, we can do something never before seen in the history of this country: win the American revolution and realize our survival as one people.

No longer in his bassinet, Four—my son—comfortably falls to sleep each nap and each night to the humming of an elephant-shaped white noise machine a mere few feet from his crib. I watch him on the baby monitor lying on his back holding his "lovey" and just babbling away in the dark as the white noise machine sounds its uninterrupted tones. Before he ultimately succumbs to sleep for the evening, he babbles loudly and assertively into the air.

What a curious scene I watch each night as Four yaps away when the white noise is supposed to put him to sleep and quiet the noises around him. "What is he doing in there?" I ask. He is talking over the white noise.

In Western culture, we sideline babbling babies to the edges of cognitive awareness and linguistic recognition. For us, babies lack clear verbal communicative facility. They can't talk, we say. According to the Beng people of West Africa—the dominant population in Côte d'Ivoire—babies arrive into this world from the eternal domain of the ancestors. The cultural contours of this rich tradition honor the genius of these young lives, a state of being from whence we all emerge. Babies live an especially spiritual life as they navigate from the realm of the ancestors into this world, which is theirs to reset and repair. In this tradition, which is not my own, my son is not just babbling to empty space in a dark room. He is talking to life unseen, the ancestral, the never gone. He has a proficiency in a language I have seemingly long forgotten.

Maybe my son does not just babble and yap to nothing. I don't know if he is talking to the dark, the ancestors, or both. All I witness is my son fighting sleep while talking over the white noise.

That's an image of the work of reparative intercession—talking over the white noise and fighting the sleep on which the survival of racism so desperately depends.

Teach Us to Pray

Great Mothering Spirit,

We enter the threshold of a new day longing for fewer reasons to be anxious and aggressive. On the wings of this demanding moment, we reach for dispositions of gratitude for personal growth and disciplined urgency to witness the toppling of the lie of race. If possible, God, remove the blinders that stop us from seeing the brilliance of the divinity of difference.

Deliver us from our rationalized reluctance to see ourselves as we are. Steady our faith in humanity, ours and all others, as we courageously own our interdependence in a posture of neighborliness. God, nurture the preexisting goodness living beneath our surface and make us sensitive to the ways we get in the way of repair.

May we open our eyes to our birthright gifts, the intangibles that verify our origins in you. We do not yet know who we are, our truest selves that are discernible only at the center of our being, where you take up residency.

God of freedom, stir within our hearts a self-patience as we pursue this journey of discomfort and confrontation, reparation and reconstruction, without cowering in our excuses.

Amen.

NOTES

Introduction Why We Are Lulled to Racial Inaction

1. Walter Earl Fluker, *The Ground Has Shifted: The Future of the Black Church in Post-Racial America* (New York: New York University Press, 2016), 22.

2. Parker Palmer, *The Politics of the Brokenhearted: On Holding the Tensions of Democracy* (Kalamazoo, MI: Fetzer Institute, 2005), 23.

3. Christopher Ingraham, "Three Quarters of Whites Don't Have Any Non-White Friends," *Washington Post*, November 25, 2021, https://www.washington post.com/news/wonk/wp/2014/08/25/three-quarters-of-whites-dont-have-any -non-white-friends/.

4. Zora Neale Hurston, quoted in Lama Rod Owens, *Love and Rage: The Path of Liberation through Anger* (Berkeley: North Atlantic Books, 2020), 277.

5. Ibram X. Kendi, *How to Be an Antiracist* (New York: One World, 2019), 9.

6. Howard Thurman, *Jesus and the Disinherited* (Boston: Beacon, 1996), 11.

7. Parker Palmer, *A Hidden Wholeness: The Journey Toward an Undivided Life* (San Francisco: Jossey-Bass, 2009), 175.

8. Parker Palmer, "The Tragic Gap," Center for Courage & Renewal, April 25, 2014, http://couragerenewal.org/the-tragic-gap/.

9. Michel Foucault, "The Meaning and Evolution of the Word 'Parrhesia': Discourse and Truth, Problematization of Parrhesia," from six lectures given by Michel Foucault at the University of California at Berkeley, October–November 1983, https://foucault.info/parrhesia/foucault.DT1.wordParrhesia.en/.

10. Foucault, "Meaning and Evolution of the Word 'Parrhesia.'"

11. Foucault, "Meaning and Evolution of the Word 'Parrhesia.'"

12. Derald Wing Sue, *Race Talk and the Conspiracy of Silence: Understanding and Facilitating Difficult Dialogues on Race* (Hoboken, NJ: John Wiley & Sons, 2015), 24.

13. Foucault, "Meaning and Evolution of the Word 'Parrhesia.'"

14. James Cone, *God of the Oppressed* (Maryknoll, NY: Orbis Books, 2012), 207.

15. Jennifer Harvey, *Dear White Christians: For Those Still Longing for Racial Reconciliation* (Grand Rapids: Eerdmans, 2014), 73.

16. Harvey, *Dear White Christians*, 159–72.

17. Harvey, *Dear White Christians*, 133.

Chapter 1 Cues to Color: Embracing Difference as Gift

1. Anthea Butler, *White Evangelical Racism: The Politics of Morality in America* (Chapel Hill: University of North Carolina Press, 2021), 58.

2. Eduardo Bonilla-Silva, *Racism without Racists: Color-Blind Racism and the Persistence of Racial Inequality in the United States*, 2nd ed. (New York: Rowman & Littlefield, 2006), 53–76.

3. Bonilla-Silva, *Racism without Racists*, 64.

4. A national phenomenon of racially restrictive clauses included in property deeds designed to keep non-Whites—and Black people in particular—from buying land.

5. Cornel West, *Prophesy Deliverance! An Afro-American Revolutionary Christianity* (Louisville: Westminster John Knox, 2002).

6. In short, those within the natural sciences validated and propagated the classification of humans into a hierarchy based on phenotypic characteristics, typically skin color, and the Renaissance and Enlightenment ideals proliferated classical Greek beauty as the uncontested standard—the intellectual seeds of White supremacist logic.

7. George D. Kelsey, *Racism and the Christian Understanding of Man* (New York: Charles Scribners' Sons, 1965), 21.

8. Kelsey, *Racism and the Christian Understanding of Man*, 27.

9. Paul Tillich, *Dynamics of Faith* (New York: Perennial, 2001), 18.

10. Paul Tillich, *Systematic Theology* (Chicago: University of Chicago Press, 2012), 1:13.

11. Paul Tillich, *Political Expectation* (Macon, GA: Mercer University Press, 1981), 41.

12. West, *Prophesy Deliverance!*, 54.

13. Tillich, *Political Expectation*, 121.

14. Paul Tillich, "You Are Accepted," in *The Essential Tillich: An Anthology of the Writings of Paul Tillich*, ed. F. Forrester Church (Chicago: University of Chicago Press, 1999), 195.

15. Kelsey, *Racism and the Christian Understanding of Man*, 33.

16. Kelsey, *Racism and the Christian Understanding of Man*, 104.

17. Peggy McIntosh, "White Privilege: Unpacking the Invisible Knapsack," in *Race, Class, and Gender: An Anthology*, ed. Margaret L. Andersen and Patricia Hill Collins, 5th ed. (Belmont, CA: Wadsworth, 2004), 104.

18. Desmond Tutu, *No Future without Forgiveness* (New York: Crown Publishing Group, 2009), 31.

19. James Baldwin, "Antisemitism and Black Power," in *The Cross of Redemption: Uncollected Writings*, ed. Randall Kenan (New York: Pantheon Books, 2010), 251.

20. James Baldwin, "A Conversation with James Baldwin," American Archive of Public Broadcasting, 1963. https://americanarchive.org/catalog/cpb-aacip_15 -0v89g5gf5r.

21. James W. Perkinson, *White Theology: Outing Supremacy in Modernity* (New York: Palgrave MacMillan, 2004), 226.

22. James Baldwin, "Antisemitism and Black Power," 251.

23. James Samuel Logan, *Good Punishment?: Christian Moral Practice and U.S. Imprisonment* (Grand Rapids: Eerdmans, 2008), 79.

24. Emmanuel Levinas, "Dialogue with Emmanuel Levinas," in *Face to Face with Levinas*, ed. Richard A. Cohen (Albany: SUNY Press, 2012), 24.

Chapter 2 Momentum to Encounter: Confronting the Histories of Whiteness

1. James Baldwin, "The White Problem," in *The Cross of Redemption: Uncollected Writings*, ed. Randall Kenan (New York: Pantheon Books, 2010), 76.

2. Charles Mills, *The Racial Contract* (Ithaca, NY: Cornell University Press, 1997), 8.

3. David Walker, *David Walker's Appeal, in Four Articles: Together with a Preamble, to the Coloured Citizens of the World, but in Particular, and Very Expressly, to Those of the United States of America: Third and Last Edition, Revised and Published by David Walker, 1830* (Halethorpe, MD: Black Classic Press, 1993), 57.

4. Barna Group, *Where Do We Go from Here?: How U.S. Christians Feel about Racism—and What They Believe It Will Take to Move Forward* (Ventura, CA: Barna Group, 2019), 45.

5. Valid Lazar Puhalo, quoted in Jeremy Myers, *Dying to Religion and Empire: Giving Up Our Religious Rites and Legal Rights* (Dallas, OR: Redeeming Press, 2018), 5.

6. Frank Newport, "Religious Group Voting and the 2020 Election," *Gallup*, November 13, 2020, https://news.gallup.com/opinion/polling-matters/324410 /religious-group-voting-2020-election.aspx.

7. Sarah Pulliam Bailey, "White Evangelicals Voted Overwhelmingly for Donald Trump, Exit Polls Show," *Washington Post*, November 9, 2016, https://www .washingtonpost.com/news/acts-of-faith/wp/2016/11/09/exit-polls-show-white -evangelicals-voted-overwhelmingly-for-donald-trump/.

8. Katie Reilly, "Here Are All the Times Donald Trump Insulted Mexico," *Time*, August 31, 2016, https://time.com/4473972/donald-trump-mexico-meeting -insult/?amp=true.

9. Stef W. Kight, "Report: Trump Said Haitian Immigrants 'All Have Aids,'" *Axios*, December 23, 2017, https://www.axios.com/report-trump-said-haitian -immigrants-all-have-aids-1515110820-4d6f7da4-ca7a-4e01-9329-7f25b49e709c .html.

10. Michael D. Shear and Julie Hirschfeld Davis, "Stoking Fears, Trump Defied Bureaucracy to Advance Immigration Agenda (Published 2017)," *New York Times*, January 4, 2018, https://www.nytimes.com/2017/12/23/us/politics/trump -immigration.amp.html?referringSource=articleShare.

11. Ibram X. Kendi, "The Day *Sh–hole* Entered the Presidential Lexicon," *The Atlantic*, January 13, 2019, https://amp.theatlantic.com/amp/article/580054/.

12. Michael O. Emerson and Christian Smith, *Divided by Faith: Evangelical Religion and the Problem of Race in America* (New York: Oxford University Press, 2000). Although the research for *Divided by Faith* paints the picture of White American evangelical religion more than two decades ago, their presentation of the historical trajectory of White evangelicals in America suggests minimal deviation has occurred.

13. Emerson and Smith, *Divided by Faith*, 3.

14. Emerson and Smith, *Divided by Faith*, 76–80.

15. "The bad news is that White Americans are still likely to blame African Americans for inequality, focusing on explanations like a lack of effort and hard work or a deficiency in African American family upbringing or culture. And they are unlikely to favor solutions that take the form of governmental intervention to 'balance the scales,' such as affirmative action or direct transfer of economic resources." See Penny Edgell and Eric Tranby, "Religious Influences on Understandings of Racial Inequality in the United States," *Social Problems* 54, no. 2 (2007): 263.

16. Emerson and Smith, *Divided by Faith*, 102

17. Emerson and Smith, *Divided by Faith*, 102.

18. Barna Group, "White Christians Have Become Even Less Motivated to Address Racial Injustice," https://www.barna.com/research/american-christians-race-problem/.

19. Barna Group, "White Christians."

20. Barna Group, *Where Do We Go from Here?*, 33.

21. Barna Group, *Where Do We Go from Here?*, 33.

22. Maya Angelou, quoted in Robert Franklin, *Crisis in the Village: Restoring Hope in African American Communities* (Philadelphia: Fortress, 2007), 60.

23. Adolph Reed Jr., "The Retrograde Quest for Symbolic Prophets of Black Liberation," *The New Republic*, January 10, 2022, https://newrepublic.com/article/161124/retrograde-quest-symbolic-prophets-black-liberation.

24. William Waller Hening, ed., *The Statutes at Large: Being a Collection of All the Laws of Virginia* (Richmond: J & G Cochran, 1821), 2:280–81.

25. Earl Pollock, *The Supreme Court and American Democracy: Case Studies on Judicial Review and Public Policy* (Westport, CT: Greenwood Press, 2009), 22.

26. "United States v. Bhagat Singh Thind," Legal Information Institute (Cornell University), https://www.law.cornell.edu/supremecourt/text/261/204.

27. Howard Thurman, *The Search for Common Ground* (Richmond: Friends United Press, 1986), 61.

28. Emily Moss, Kriston McIntosh, Wendy Edelberg, and Kristen Broady, "The Black-White Wealth Gap Left Black Households More Vulnerable," *Brookings*, December 8, 2020, https://www.brookings.edu/blog/up-front/2020/12/08/the-black-white-wealth-gap-left-black-households-more-vulnerable/amp/.

29. Christian E. Weller and Lily Roberts, "Eliminating the Black-White Wealth Gap Is a Generational Challenge," Center for American Progress, March 19, 2021, https://www.americanprogress.org/article/eliminating-black-white-wealth-gap-generational-challenge/.

30. Calvin Schermerhorn, "Why the Racial Wealth Gap Persists, More than 150 Years after Emancipation," *Washington Post*, June 19, 2019, https://www.washingtonpost.com/outlook/2019/06/19/why-racial-wealth-gap-persists-more-than-years-after-emancipation/.

31. Michelle Alexander, *The New Jim Crow: Mass Incarceration in the Age of Colorblindness* (New York: New Press, 2010), 175.

32. Elizabeth Hinton, *From the War on Poverty to the War on Crime: The Making of Mass Incarceration* (Cambridge, MA: Harvard University Press, 2016), 5.

33. Alexander, *The New Jim Crow*, 77.

34. Kelly Brown Douglas, *Stand Your Ground: Black Bodies and the Justice of God* (Maryknoll, NY: Orbis Books, 2015), 79.

35. Khalil Gibran Muhammad, *The Condemnation of Blackness: Race, Crime, and the Making of Modern Urban America* (Cambridge: Harvard University Press, 2010), 54.

36. Muhammad, *Condemnation of Blackness*, 4.

37. Douglas, *Stand Your Ground*, 53.

38. Muhammad, *Condemnation of Blackness*, 59.

Chapter 3 Pattern Recognition: Honoring Our Interdependence

1. Patricia Hill Collins, *Black Feminist Thought: Knowledge, Consciousness, and the Politics of Empowerment* (New York: Taylor & Francis, 2002), 18.

2. Martin Luther King Jr., "Letter from a Birmingham Jail," in *Why We Can't Wait* (New York: Signet Classics, 2000), 65.

3. Cedric Robinson, *Black Marxism: The Making of the Black Radical Tradition* (Chapel Hill: The University of North Carolina Press, 2000). 9.

4. Eleven years after the signing of the Declaration of Independence, the three-fifths compromise was an arrangement between the Northern and Southern delegates of the 1787 US Constitutional Convention, which allowed slaveholding states to count enslaved Africans as three-fifths of a person. This calculation factored into direct taxation and representation in the US House of Representatives. This metric augmented the legislative power of Southern states despite slaves not having any rights or real representation in the federal legislature.

5. Chye-Ching Huang. "Fundamentally Flawed 2017 Tax Law Largely Leaves Low- and Moderate-Income Americans Behind," *Center on Budget and Policy Priorities*, February 27, 2019, https://www.cbpp.org/research/federal-tax/fundamentally-flawed-2017-tax-law-largely-leaves-low-and-moderate-income.

6. Stuart Hall et al., *Policing the Crisis: Mugging, the State and Law and Order* (New York: Macmillan, 1978), 394.

7. Robinson, *Black Marxism*, 27.

8. Robin D. G. Kelley, "What Did Cedric Robinson Mean by Racial Capitalism?," *Boston Review*, December 13, 2019, http://bostonreview.net/race/robin-d-g-kelley-what-did-cedric-robinson-mean-racial-capitalism.

9. Robinson, *Black Marxism*, 26.

10. Robinson, *Black Marxism*, 41.

11. Kelly Brown Douglas, *Stand Your Ground: Black Bodies and the Justice of God* (Maryknoll, NY: Orbis Books, 2015), 35.

12. Douglas, *Stand Your Ground*, 40.

13. Richard Wright, *Twelve Million Black Voices: A Folk History of the Negro in the United States of America* (London: L. Drummond, 1947), 43.

14. W. E. B. Du Bois, *Black Reconstruction in America, 1860–1880* (New York: Free Press, 1998), 700–701.

15. Rakesh Kochhar and Anthony Cilluffo, "How Wealth Inequality Has Changed in the U.S. since the Great Recession, by Race, Ethnicity and Income," Pew Research Center, November 1, 2017, https://www.pewresearch.org/fact -tank/2017/11/01/how-wealth-inequality-has-changed-in-the-u-s-since-the-great -recession-by-race-ethnicity-and-income/.

16. Dorothy Brown, *The Whiteness of Wealth: How the Tax System Impoverishes Black Americans—and How We Can Fix It* (New York: Crown, 2021), 209.

17. Brown, *Whiteness of Wealth*, 209.

18. Brown, *Whiteness of Wealth*, 207.

19. Otis Madison, quoted in Cedric Robinson, *Forgeries of Memory and Meaning* (Chapel Hill: University of North Carolina, 2012), 83.

20. Christopher Ingraham, "Analysis: The Richest 1 Percent Now Owns More of the Country's Wealth Than at Any Time in the Past 50 Years," *Washington Post*, November 24, 2021, https://www.washingtonpost.com/news/wonk/wp/2017 /12/06/the-richest-1-percent-now-owns-more-of-the-countrys-wealth-than-at-any -time-in-the-past-50-years/.

21. Mary Papenfuss, "400 Richest Americans Own More than 150 Million of the Nation's Poorest: Study," *HuffPost*, February 11, 2019, https://www.huff post.com/entry/400-richest-own-more-than-150-million-poorest_n_5c60f627e 4b0eec79b250c34.

22. Elizabeth Warren (@ewarren), "What's "ridiculous" is billionaires who think they can buy the presidency to keep the system rigged for themselves while opportunity slips away for everyone else. The top 0.1%, who'd pay my #UltraMillionaireTax, own about the same wealth as 90% of America. It's time for change." Twitter, January 29, 2019, 9:17 a.m., https://twitter.com/ewarren /status/1090252713156403200?s=20.

23. Institute for Policy Studies and Americans for Tax Fairness, "Billionaire Pandemic Wealth Gains of 55%, or $1.6 Trillion, Come amid Three Decades of Rapid Wealth Growth," April 15, 2021, https://inequality.org/wp-content/uploads /2021/04/IPS-ATF-Billionaires-13-Month-31-Year-Report-copy.pdf.

24. Dylan Matthews, "How the 1 Percent Won the Recovery, in One Table," *Washington Post*, April 28, 2019, https://www.washingtonpost.com/news/wonk /wp/2013/09/11/how-the-1percent-won-the-recovery-in-one-table/.

25. Matthews, "How the 1 Percent Won the Recovery."

26. Juliana Menasce Horowitz, Ruth Igielnik, and Rakesh Kochhar, "Trends in Income and Wealth Inequality," Pew Research Center, January 9, 2020, https:// www.pewresearch.org/social-trends/2020/01/09/trends-in-income-and-wealth -inequality/.

27. "In Mississippi and Virginia, [the poll tax] was cumulative for two years; if a tenant farmer or textile worker couldn't pay in any given year, not only did he miss an election cycle, he had to pay a full two years' tax to restore his voting rights. In Georgia, the poll tax was cumulative from the time a voter

turned 21 years old—meaning, if one missed 10 years, he or she would have to pay a decade's worth of back taxes before regaining the right to vote. In Texas, the tax was due on February 1, in the winter off-season, when farmers were habitually strapped for cash." See Joshua Zeitz, "Does the White Working Class Really Vote against Its Own Interests?," *Politico Magazine*, December 31, 2017, https://www.politico.com/magazine/story/2017/12/31/trump-white -working-class-history-216200/.

28. Howard Thurman, *The Luminous Darkness: A Personal Interpretation of the Anatomy of Segregation and the Ground of Hope* (Richmond, IN: Friends United Press, 1965), 6.

29. Howard Thurman, *Jesus and the Disinherited* (Boston: Beacon Press, 2012), 89.

30. Howard Thurman, "The Significance of Jesus III: Love," in *The Papers of Howard Washington Thurman*, ed. Walter Fluker (Columbia: University of South Carolina Press, 2017), 2:63.

31. Ben Witherington, *Jesus Quest: The Third Search for the Jew of Nazareth* (Downers Grove, IL: InterVarsity, 1997), 142.

32. Howard Thurman, "The American Dream," in *Papers of Howard Washington Thurman*, 4:217–18.

33. Walter Brueggemann, *Money and Possessions* (Louisville: Westminster John Knox, 2016), 51.

34. Cedric Robinson, *Terms of Order: Political Science and the Myth of Leadership* (Albany, NY: SUNY, 1980), 198.

35. Robinson, *Terms of Order*, 205.

36. Robinson, *Terms of Order*, 205.

Chapter 4 Syncopated Identity: Exploring Our Fuller Selves

1. Derald Wing Sue, *Race Talk and the Conspiracy of Silence: Understanding and Facilitating Difficult Dialogues on Race* (Hoboken, NJ: John Wiley & Sons, 2015), 7.

2. Imani Perry, *More Beautiful and More Terrible: The Embrace and Transcendence of Racial Inequality in the United States* (New York: New York University Press, 2011), 31.

3. Perry, *More Beautiful and More Terrible*, 42.

4. Amanda Barroso, "How Often People Talk about Race with Family and Friends Depends on Racial and Ethnic Group, Education, Politics," *Pew Research Center*, August 18, 2020, https://www.pewresearch.org/fact-tank/2019/06/25/how -often-people-talk-about-race-with-family-and-friends/.

5. Erica Frankenberg, Jongyeon Ee, Jennifer B. Ayscue, and Gary Orfield, "Harming Our Common Future: America's Segregated Schools 65 Years After *Brown*," The Civil Rights Project, May 10, 2019, https://www.civilrightsproject .ucla.edu/research/k-12-education/integration-and-diversity/harming-our -common-future-americas-segregated-schools-65-years-after-brown/Brown-65 -050919v4-final.pdf.

6. John Erlichman, quoted in Dan Baum, "Legalize It All: How to Win the War on Drugs," *Harper's Magazine*, August 18, 2016, 22.

7. Aaron Griffith, *God's Law and Order: The Politics of Punishment in Evangelical America* (Cambridge, MA: Harvard University Press, 2020), 91.

8. Griffith, *God's Law and Order*, 146.

9. Rick Perlstein, "Exclusive: Lee Atwater's Infamous 1981 Interview on the Southern Strategy," *Nation*, December 7, 2018, https://www.thenation.com/article/archive/exclusive-lee-atwaters-infamous-1981-interview-southern-strategy/.

10. See Sylvan Lane, "Trump Claims Decision to Repeal Fair Housing Rule Will Boost Home Prices, Lower Crime," *The Hill*, July 29, 2020, https://thehill.com/policy/finance/509595-trump-claims-decision-to-repeal-fair-housing-rule-will-boost-home-prices-lower.

11. James W. Perkinson, *White Theology: Outing Supremacy in Modernity* (New York: Palgrave MacMillan, 2004), 232.

12. When queried about the historical Jesus in a national survey of nine hundred Christians for my doctoral research, 90.9 percent indicated they understood Jesus as a spiritual leader, 86.8 percent as a social revolutionary leader, 75 percent as God incarnate, 88.9 percent as the Son of God, and 56 percent as a Hebrew prophet.

13. Audre Lorde, "Learning from the 60s," in *Sister Outsider: Essays and Speeches* (Berkeley: Crossing Press, 2007), 138.

14. Toni Morrison, "Nobel Lecture," The Nobel Prize, December 7, 1993, https://www.nobelprize.org/prizes/literature/1993/morrison/lecture/.

15. Karl Barth. quoted in Christopher Morse, *Not Every Spirit: A Dogmatics of Christian Disbelief*, 2nd ed. (New York: Continuum International Press, 2009) 18.

16. Morse, *Not Every Spirit*, 6.

17. Martin Luther King Jr.. *The Papers of Martin Luther King, Jr., Volume III: Birth of a New Age, December 1955-December 1956*, ed. Clayborne Carson. (Berkeley: University of California Press, 1992), 460.

Chapter 5 Pulse to Risk: Sacrificing Our Power and Privilege

1. James Baldwin, *The Fire Next Time* (New York: Vintage International, 1993), 34.

2. John Welwood, quoted in Larry Yang, *Awakening Together: The Spiritual Practice of Inclusivity and Community* (Somerville, MA: Wisdom Publications, 2017), 90.

3. Anna Julia Cooper, *The Voice of Anna Julia Cooper: Including a Voice from the South and Other Important Essays, Papers, and Letters* (New York: Rowman & Littlefield, 2000), 106.

4. Peter Gomes, *The Scandalous Gospel of Jesus: What's So Good About the Gospel?* (New York: HarperOne, 2009), 66.

5. Michel Foucault, "Truth and Power," in *The Essential Works of Foucault*, ed. James D. Faubion (New York: The New Press, 2000), 3:132–33.

6. Obery Hendricks, *The Politics of Jesus: Rediscovering the True Revolutionary Nature of the Teachings of Jesus and How They Have Been Corrupted* (New York: Three Leaves Press, 2006), 71.

7. Hendricks, *Politics of Jesus*, 72–73.

8. Ida B. Wells-Barnett, *Southern Horrors: Lynch Law in All Its Phases* (Frankfurt: Outlook, 2018), 2.

9. Kerry Walters, *Harriet Tubman: A Life in American History* (Santa Barbara: ABC-CLIO, 2019), 94.

10. Julius Crump and Peter Paris, *African American Theological Ethics: A Reader* (Louisville: Westminster John Knox, 2015), 33.

11. Willie Francois, "A Tree with Roots: Probing American History to Situate an Abolitionist Approach to Crisis," in *Abolitionist Leadership in Schools: Undoing Systemic Injustice through Communally Conscious Education*, ed. Robert Harvey (New York: Taylor & Francis Group, 2021), 37–38.

12. Hendricks, *Politics of Jesus*, 109.

13. Tim Stafford, "The Abolitionists," *Christianity Today*, January 1, 1992, https://www.christianitytoday.com/history/issues/issue-33/abolitionists.html.

14. George Beach, *Transforming Liberalism: The Theology of James Luther Adams* (Boston: Skinner House Books, 2005), 185.

15. bell hooks, "Love as the Practice of Freedom," in *Outlaw Culture: Resisting Representations* (New York: Routledge, 1994), 293.

16. William Lloyd Garrison, "I Am an Abolitionist" (1841), in *Let Justice Be Done: Writings from American Abolitionists, 1688–1865*, ed. Kerry Walters (Maryknoll, NY: Orbis Books, 2020), 85.

17. James Cone, *God of the Oppressed* (Maryknoll, NY: Orbis Books, 1997), 134.

18. Leah Gunning Francis, *Ferguson and Faith: Sparking Leadership and Awakening Community* (St. Louis: Chalice Press, 2015), 91.

19. James Alfred Smith and Brooks Berndt, *Sounding the Trumpet: How Churches Can Answer God's Call to Justice* (Boiling Springs, NC: A Pair of Docs, 2013), 68–69.

20. Dom Helder Camara, quoted in Jamie Arpin-Ricci, *The Cost of Community: Jesus, St. Francis, and Life in the Kingdom* (Downers Grove, IL: Intervarsity, 2011), 159.

21. Toni Morrison, *Beloved* (New York: Vintage International, 2007), 103.

22. Andrew K. Franklin, "King in 1967: My Dream Has 'Turned into a Nightmare,'" *NBC News*, August 27, 2013, https://www.nbcnews.com/nightly-news/king-1967-my-dream-has-turned-nightmare-flna8c11013179.

23. Willie James Jennings, *The Christian Imagination: Theology and the Origins of Race* (New Haven: Yale University Press, 2010), 6.

24. Percy Bysshe Shelley, "A Defence of Poetry," Poetry Foundation, October 13, 2009, https://www.poetryfoundation.org/articles/69388/a-defence-of-poetry.

25. Eddie Glaude, "America Is Suffering a Crisis of Imagination," *Time*, February 24, 2016, https://time.com/4235720/democrats-sanders-clinton-black-voters/.

26. See Caroline Hartzell and Matthew Hoddie, *Power Sharing and Democracy in Post–Civil War States: The Art of the Possible* (New York: Cambridge University Press, 2020), 82.

27. Frederick Douglass, *West India Emancipation* (Glasglow, UK: Good Press, 2020), 14.

28. Robert Harvey, *Abolitionist Leadership in Schools: Undoing Systemic Injustice through Communally Conscious Education* (New York: Taylor & Francis Group, 2021), 23.

Chapter 6 Downbeat Truth: Naming Our Complicity in Racism

1. Tom McCarthy, "Amy Coney Barrett Is a Constitutional 'Originalist' – but What Does It Mean?," *The Guardian* (October 27, 2020), https://www.theguardian.com/us-news/2020/oct/26/amy-coney-barrett-originalist-but-what-does-it-mean.

2. Howard Thurman, *Essential Writings* (Maryknoll, NY: Orbis Books, 2006), 141.

3. Robert Kennedy, quoted in Brian Thomsen, *The Dream That Will Not Die: Inspiring Words of John, Robert, and Edward Kennedy* (New York: Tom Doherty Associates, 2010), 126–27.

4. Hearing Before the Subcommittee on Constitution, Civil Rights and Human Rights of the Committee on the Judiciary, United States Senate, One Hundred Twelfth Congress, Second Session, December 12, 2012, (Washington, DC: US Government Printing Office, 2012), 679. Available online at http://www.govinfo.gov/content/pkg/CHRG-112shrg86166/pdf/CHRG-112shrg86166.pdf.

5. Elizabeth Shively, "Commentary on Philippians 2:5–11," *Working Preacher*, Luther Seminary, March 24, 2013, https://www.workingpreacher.org/commentaries/revised-common-lectionary/sunday-of-the-passion-palm-sunday-3/commentary-on-philippians-25-11-6.

6. Mahatma Gandhi, *The Collected Works of Mahatma Gandhi* (India: Publications Division, Ministry of Information and Broadcasting, Government of India, 1965), 18:195.

7. Josiah Royce, *Philosophy of Loyalty* (New York: SophiaOmni, 2017), 18.

8. Royce, *Philosophy of Loyalty*, 55.

9. Royce, *Philosophy of Loyalty*, 119.

10. Josiah Royce, *The Problem of Christianity* (Washington, DC: University of America Press, 2001), 140.

11. Josiah Royce, quoted in Kipton Jensen, "The Growing Edges of Beloved Community: From Royce to Thurman and King," *Transactions of the Charles S. Peirce Society* 52, no. 3 (Spring 2016): 242.

12. Henry Mayer, *All on Fire: William Lloyd Garrison and the Abolition of Slavery* (New York: Norton, 2008), xv.

13. Mayer, *All on Fire*, 267.

Conclusion Invent Hope Every Day

1. Eddie Glaude, *Begin Again: James Baldwin's America and Its Urgent Lessons for Our Own* (New York: Crown, 2020), 145.

2. Jenkin Lloyd Jones, *Love for the Battle-Torn Peoples Sermon Study* (Chicago: Unity, 2016), 115.

3. Cornel West, *Race Matters* (Boston: Beacon, 2001), 14.

4. Martin Luther King Jr., "Love, Law, Civil Disobedience," in *A Testament of Hope* (New York: Harper One, 2003), 52.

5. James Cone, *The Spirituals and the Blues: An Interpretation* (Maryknoll, NY: Orbis Books, 1991), 31.

6. David Arnold, *August Wilson: A Casebook* (New York: Garland Publishing, 2000), 202.

7. A photo of this painting is available at https://www.kunstarchive.net/en /wvz/samuel_bak/works/act_of_balance/type/all.

8. Michel Foucault, *The History of Sexuality*, trans. Robert Hurley (New York: Vintage Books, 2012), 95.

9. Michel de Certeau, *The Practice of Everyday Life*, trans. Steven Randall (Berkeley: University of California Press, 1984), 38.

10. De Certeau, *Practice of Everyday Life*, 37.

11. De Certeau, *Practice of Everyday Life*, 37.

12. Thomas Merton, *No Man Is an Island* (Boston: Shambhala, 2005), 123.

Willie Dwayne Francois III (DMin, Candler School of Theology) serves as senior pastor of Mount Zion Baptist Church in Pleasantville, New Jersey, and president of the Black Church Center for Justice and Equality. Francois is the director of the Master of Professional Studies Program at Sing Sing Correctional Facility and assistant professor of liberation theology at New York Theological Seminary. A graduate of Morehouse College and Harvard Divinity School, he created the Public Love Organizing and Training (PLOT) project and has served in various organizations engaging issues of racial justice, including the Atlantic City chapter of Black Lives Matter, the Samuel DeWitt Proctor Conference, the Progressive National Baptist Convention, Inc., Community Change, and the New Jersey Department of State's MLK Jr. Commission. He has written for *Huff Post*, *The Hill*, *The Christian Century*, *Sojourners*, and *Religion Dispatches* and enjoys a busy speaking schedule. As an abolitionist, Francois practices pastoral activism around racial equity, economic justice, and radical legal system and education reform.